WHO'S TO BLAME?

Escape the Victim Trap & Gain Personal Power in Your Relationships

CARMEN RENEE BERRY, MSW
& MARK W. BAKER, PhD

PIÑON PRESS

P.O. Box 35007, Colorado Springs, CO 80935

Library of Congress Catalog Card Number:
   96-33642
ISBN 08910-99158

Cover illustration: Eileen Dailey/Stock Illustration
Source Inc.

Some of the anecdotal illustrations in this book are
true to life and are included with the permission of
the persons involved. All other illustrations are
composites of real situations, and any resemblance
to people living or dead is coincidental.

This publication is designed to provide accurate and
authoritative information in regard to the subject
matter covered. It is sold with the understanding that
the author and the publisher are not engaged in ren-
dering legal, accounting, or other professional service.
If legal advice or other expert assistance is required,
the services of a competent professional person
should be sought. *From a Declaration of Principles
jointly adopted by a Committee of the American Bar
Association and a Committee of Publishers.*

Berry, Carmen Renee.
   Who's to blame? : escape the victim trap and
gain personal power in your relationships /
Carmen Renee Berry and Mark W. Baker.
      p.   cm.
   ISBN 0-89109-915-8 (paper)
   1. Adjustment (Psychology) 2. Psychic trauma.
3. Victims—Psychology. 4. Self-defeating behavior.
5. Blame. I. Baker, Mark W., Ph.D. II. Title.
BF335.4.B47   1996
158' .2—dc20   96-33642
                                       CIP

Printed in the United States of America

1 2 3 4 5 6 7 8 9 10 / 99 98 97 96

CONTENTS

To Phillip Baker,
for teaching me more about genuine powerlessness
and power than anyone else in my life
MWB

To Catherine Smith and Bob Parsons
who, over the years, empowered me with their
understanding, acceptance, and wisdom
CRB

1

THE
VICTIM TRAP

ALICIA STILL HAD the gun in her hand when the police arrived. Looking down at her husband lying in a pool of blood, all she could do was cry. How did it ever get this bad? No one was there to help, and she had to do something to stop him. She had to make sure he wouldn't beat her ever again.

Who's to blame? The husband who beat his wife or the woman who pulled the trigger?

～

Allen watched from his car as Janie walked into the restaurant. Through the window he could see her as she sat down with a handsome man at a table for two. Fuming, Allen leaped out of his car and stormed into the restaurant. How could Janie go out on him behind his back like this? He had every intention of breaking up her little rendezvous.

Who's to blame? The man who creates an embarrassing public scene or the woman who betrays his trust?

～

Lillie begged her husband not to leave. It was beyond comprehension how he could abandon her with their two-year-old daughter and a baby on the way. She vowed never to let him see his children again if he left her. In her mind he would be giving up his rights as a parent.

Who's to blame? The man who abandons his wife or the woman who tries to control him by using their children?

~

Who's to blame when people get hurt by others who have been hurt as well? In our seminars and in our work as therapists over the past fifteen years, we have observed an increasing tendency among some people in our society to use the label of "victim" to justify hurting other people. Rather than breaking the cycle of abuse, such justifications perpetuate the damage people cause each other. One hurting person hurts another, who then hurts another person, renewing the cycle. Getting to the bottom of this conundrum of hurt and blame can be pretty tricky. If you have been in a hurtful relationship like this, you have probably wanted to yell, "Just stop it!" on a number of occasions, because you didn't know what else to say and you couldn't tell whose fault it was anyway. If you find yourself wondering "How did I ever get into this mess?" here are some ideas that may help to answer this question.

We enter into most relationships hoping to find intimacy based on a shared sense of reality. This means our perceptions of the world are shared by the other, and even when we disagree, we can come to a common understanding about why we disagree and then accept our differences.

Good relationships are mutually beneficial, and often intense, positive emotions are associated with just being together. If all goes well, we even feel appreciated and needed. This initial stage of a relationship can be rewarding and fun and can make us feel good about ourselves.

Then something happens that is inevitable in every relationship. A conflict arises and it becomes necessary to clarify our perspectives on the problem. We discover that we do not completely share the same perspective on reality we thought we did. If the conflict is severe enough, it disrupts the blissful and harmonious intimacy we experienced. We look at one another and wonder, "Who is this person *really*?" We feel separated and anxious to regain a sense of commonality, mutuality, and understanding.

So we launch into a "negotiation" stage in which we try to convince the other of our perspective on reality. In healthy relationships, differences in perceptions can be discussed, sometimes resolved, and hopefully always tolerated. Some changes in the relationship's boundaries, definition, or expectations may be necessary, but the changes usually result in a new balance of shared power. We then relax into a newly established shared reality until the next inevitable conflict arises.

Some relationships, unfortunately, do not accommodate differences and change. The views of reality differ so greatly that one person may feel as if he or she is relating to an alien from another planet. If one or both of the individuals operates from a perspective of powerlessness, a new level of equilibrium can be extremely difficult, if not impossible, to achieve. The relationship then falls into the Victim Trap.

The Victim Trap operates when people believe they are personally powerless. The dynamic of powerlessness causes people to mismanage their emotions through blame. Anyone can fall into the Victim Trap, and most of us have at some time in our lives. Ironically, the trap is not filled with people in crisis, though the people who find themselves ensnared typically bounce from one problematic encounter to another. Rather, it is filled with people who chronically operate with the belief that at least one of the people in the relationship lacks personal power.

WHO GETS CAUGHT IN THE TRAP?

Some people undergo the worst forms of abuse and suffering, yet they seem to turn out relatively well and go on to live productive lives. Other people experience abuse or trauma and become so devastated by it that they carry the memories and the effect with them for the rest of their lives. Simply put, some people get better and others get bitter. Some people manage their emotional lives quite effectively; others mismanage them terribly. Some people survive victimizing experiences in ways that result in healing and regaining a sense of personal power. Others chronically blame people, forfeit their sense of power, and mismanage their most potent emotions. Why do the former avoid the Victim Trap, but the latter get caught in it?

There are two ways to fall into the Victim Trap. First, you fall into the trap by failing to believe in your own personal power, seeing circumstances and/or other people as controlling your life. Any of us can fall into this trap because we have all been victimized in some way. Victimization is wrong or harmful treatment when we can't defend ourselves. No one escapes some degree of hurt or misunderstanding. The question we believe people need to be asking is not, "Have I ever been hurt?" but, "How will I respond when I am hurt?"

Consider our example of Allen, the man who caused a scene in the restaurant when he saw Janie, the woman he was dating, with another man. Allen fell into the Victim Trap when he relinquished his power over his own sense of well-being, believing he could only be happy if Janie loved him. He felt utterly dependent upon Janie for feeling worth-

8

while, safe, strong, and manly. Rather than managing his own emotions effectively and creating a relationship with Janie in which power was shared equally, Allen was consumed with controlling her and making her love him. Feeling powerless, he acted out in powerfully demonstrative ways. Allen's disruptive display in the restaurant made him feel powerful for a brief moment, but originated from the belief that he was desperately vulnerable to Janie's rejection.

While you may never have made a public spectacle of yourself like Allen, if you've ever believed your sense of happiness or well-being was defined by someone else's behavior, you've fallen into the trap. Our society supports this way of thinking, by helping us blame unfair love relationships, childhood abuse, parental abandonment, or emotional or sexual trauma for all of our painful emotions, behaviors, and choices. We may hate the fact that a particular event or person ever existed in our lives, but nevertheless, we allow that person or event to define our identities.

A second way to fall into the trap can be seen in Janie's reaction to Allen's public outburst. When Allen bolted into the restaurant, accusing her of betrayal, Janie took responsibility for his pain and for calming him down. Because there was some truth to his accusations, she took total responsibility for his emotions and actions. She excused herself and led Allen outside where he began to cry, blaming his behavior on his love for her. Rather than telling Allen that she was not interested in this kind of love, Janie saw herself as the reason he was emotionally unstable, vowing to do a better job in the future of being worthy of his love.

Like Janie, we fall into the Victim Trap when we maintain a relationship with an adult we believe to be powerless or significantly less powerful than we believe ourselves to be. Janie saw herself as the powerful one in the relationship, needing to stay within the narrow confines of Allen's demands in order to keep him emotionally stabilized. Whenever any of us feels responsible for another adult's actions or emotional well-being, we are slipping into the trap.

You may know people who see themselves as powerless because of some past abuse, and you may have fallen into the trap by believing they are powerless as well. Rarely is this shared perspective on reality openly discussed. In fact, you may not even realize that you view these people as powerless. All you may know is that there is something uncomfortable, if not downright painful, about these relationships. You may feel powerfully drawn and yet terribly confused.

When involved in such a relationship, you probably feel misunderstood, criticized, and even trapped. You may try to understand the painful circumstances that cause the person to feel victimized by others, or possibly by you, but your efforts to make things better are just not enough. In fact, you probably feel as if you are being judged for not doing your part in the relationship—that somehow it is your fault things aren't getting better.

It is often quite difficult to recognize that a relationship is ensnared in the Victim Trap, but over time a pattern of behavior emerges that establishes whether or not this is a healthy relationship for you. The place to begin is with yourself as you observe yourself and those with whom you relate. The following pages may help you decide whether or not you have fallen into the Victim Trap, either by discounting your personal power or by trying to relate to someone who no longer believes he or she is powerful.

FALLING INTO THE VICTIM TRAP
BY DISCOUNTING YOUR PERSONAL POWER

None of us comes to the belief that we are powerless by ourselves. Often we repress our personal power because important people in our lives responded to our assertion of power in a negative way. All of us are especially impressionable during our childhood years, and we often develop lifelong attitudes about ourselves as a result of how we were treated then. For some, the expression of power was not received well by others during childhood. Perhaps our parents thought it was improper, or our schoolteachers thought it was disorderly, or our minister thought it was self-centered, but somehow we got the message that being powerful was a bad thing. In fact, a whole society can send a message about how wrong it is for us to believe we are powerful if we do not fit that society's definition of a person entitled to such power. If we are told enough times that we have no right to power, even if we're not aware of getting that message, we can start to believe it.

The most crippling part of developing a sense of personal powerlessness is not just that others responded negatively to us, but that we had to deal with it by ourselves. No one was there to say they understood, to talk about it, or to just be with us. Without that kind of support we were unable to make any sense out of what was happening to us. A knowing look, an empathic word, or a sympathetic presence might have made all the difference. But support rarely, if ever, came.

We take what we learn as children into adulthood. If taught to see ourselves as powerless, we will not use our personal power to protect ourselves from harm. Consequently, we often experience a great deal of unnecessary and unproductive suffering. Suffering can be productive as a necessary part of anyone's learning experience. When we make a mistake, pain often results, which serves as an indicator of error. If we allow suffering to be our teacher, we can learn to change our behavior, our perspectives or opinions, and avoid repeating the same painful mistakes.

11

When we are locked into a posture of powerlessness, however, our suffering is unproductive and does not result in growth. Rather than using pain as a motivator to accurately examine our lives, assume responsibility for our choices, and use our personal power for change, we often glorify the experience of suffering itself. Suffering is always unproductive when we're caught in the Victim Trap. For example, Allen mistook his emotional suffering as an indication of his love for Janie, rather than as an indication that he was mismanaging his emotions. When Allen stormed into the restaurant he did not notice the pain Janie experienced as a signal to examine the power imbalance that existed between them. Janie and Allen saw the incident as a badge of honor, an indication of the greatness of their love and the strength of their relationship. Their suffering was used as a confirmation of their love, rather than a warning that something was terribly amiss.

Another way we fail to understand what suffering can teach us is by believing that our needs are secondary to others'. Janie fell prey to this thinking when she felt that the pain she suffered was somehow helpful to Allen. Her embarrassment in the restaurant, her feeling cut off from relationships with other men, her anxiety about whether or not she was "making" Allen happy were endured as sacrifices to their relationship. Since Janie had never learned that her needs and feelings had merit, the pain she experienced with Allen felt "right" and familiar.

Many of us fall into this trap. If we have been disregarded or used, we can believe that the suffering of others is more important than our own pain. Drawing attention to our own needs is then seen as shameful and a sign of a moral defect. To be needy is to be pathetic, so paying attention to our own pain or needing anything from anyone because of our pain is viewed as pitiful. The experience of having our feelings matter to others is missing; consequently, the sense that we matter as people is missing as well. Because of this, those of us in the Victim Trap never develop a sense of personal efficacy, and we conclude early on that we lack something inside that other people have which enables them to be happy. We view ourselves as needy rather than having needs, so we rarely have relationships in which our legitimate needs are expressed and satisfied. This cycle of neediness, shame, and more unmet needs only confirms that we are, indeed, powerless people.

When we believe we are powerless, it is very difficult for us to tolerate differences in perspective. As a result, navigating and negotiating conflict becomes almost impossible. We do not believe we will ever get what we need unless others see things the way we do. We become entrenched in our perspective on reality and consequently subtly coerce others to conform to it. Attempts to negotiate a new shared reality, one that includes some differences, is perceived as a threat.

Rather than grow more secure in his relationship with Janie, Allen became more and more jealous as time went on. Janie tried every way she could to convince Allen that she loved him, and him only. She accounted for every minute of her time, stopped spending time with her girlfriends and even allowed him to drive her back and forth to work. But nothing Janie could do would soothe Allen's fears. Janie was living like a caged animal with Allen as her keeper.

Neither Allen or Janie were consciously aware of how disturbed their relationship had become. The roots of their problem sank deep into their unconscious and were out of their conscious view. Needs, motivations, and feelings that are largely influenced by unconscious forces are often dangerous to ourselves and to those with whom we relate. The more we try to help, the more harm we cause. The more we work for clarity, the more confusion we experience. The more we try to protect ourselves, the more we put ourselves in jeopardy.

THE POWER IN THE UNCONSCIOUS

Survival is an inherent value shared by all living creatures. In order to survive, the human mind protects us from dealing with experiences of pain that we are emotionally or physically unable to handle. As a consequence, certain memories, feelings, and thoughts are held in the unconscious part of ourselves. When aspects of life are too distressing to think about, they are often relegated to the unconscious or they are physically stored in the body.

A metaphor for how this takes place is the three states of water. Although it is essentially the same chemical, two parts hydrogen to one part oxygen, water can exist in the form of liquid, solid, or gas. In all three states it is still water, but it looks and acts differently, depending upon which state it is in. Emotions can exist in various states in much the same way. Feelings can be intentionally expressed when they are in the conscious state of mind, but when those same emotions are held in the unconscious state of mind, their influence is much different. It is also possible for emotions to exist physically rather than mentally or emotionally, in the form of muscle tension, pain, or even illness. The same emotion can move between all three states depending upon how threatening it is to us. Just because an emotion may not be able to be articulated verbally does not preclude it from being stored somewhere in the mind or body.

You may have experienced this yourself in the past. Have you ever been angry at someone to whom you could not express it? Perhaps a boss, a teacher or a relative has done something to hurt you, but it would not be appropriate to

14

communicate how angry you are about it. If you got a headache at this point, it is very likely that your anger was expressing itself in bodily form. If someone confronted you with something like "I'll bet you're really mad now," and you barked back at them in a hostile tone "I'm not angry, that didn't bother me at all!" then your tone of voice may be betraying the fact that your anger is residing in an unconscious form in your mind. But if you fumed silently until you could get in your car where you could scream at the top of your lungs, that would be the conscious form of expressing your anger. All three experiences of anger are just as real, even though they appear in three different forms.

Most everyone in our society understands that their dreams during sleep tell them something about themselves that they can't quite grasp when awake. It has become a part of common speech to point out a "Freudian slip" to anyone who mixes up their words to betray a deeper meaning they unknowingly might be communicating. And who hasn't tried to remember something that, even though it was on the "tip of the tongue," couldn't quite be recalled until someone helped them out? All of these experiences point us to the human unconscious. Even though it isn't really a physical part of the brain, the unconscious is thought of as the place where we keep thoughts and feelings that are not allowed into our conscious life. This psychological process protects us from dangerous memories that might threaten our normal daily lives. Without the unconscious, we would have to deal with everything that ever troubled us all at once, which would be a task too difficult to manage.

It is normal not to be aware of all our thoughts or feelings on a particular subject. Our unconscious may hold disturbing matters that would distract rather than help us at any given moment. The fact that we have an unconscious is not a problem; denying that we have one is. Not wanting to know what is in our unconscious, and only wanting to deal with the obvious meanings of things, leads to superficial understandings of ourselves and our behavior.

When we hold beliefs about ourselves in our unconscious, we believe them as though they were the absolute truth. Those who repress feelings of personal power are not thinking they might be inadequate; they are *convinced* that they are inadequate. A panicked desperation results. They fear they have no power to control anything.

When operating out of a sense of powerlessness, we fail to recognize the significant influence of our past relationships on our reactions to current pain. Our childhood, previous relationships, and years of conditioning affect every response we have today. We mistakenly believe we do not have the ability to deal with our memories, so we try to avoid them as much as possible, only to be controlled by unconscious forces we rarely understand. Thus, we become reactors to our memories rather than actors informed by our memories.

When we get caught in the Victim Trap, we deny or minimize the impact of the unconscious. We have an investment in keeping painful feelings out of conscious awareness because we are too afraid to explore what might come up. The Victim Trap motto is "Don't go digging up what's dead and buried." The problem is, many things have been buried alive. Issues and events that might evoke strong feelings are just as "alive" as they were when relegated to the unconscious, but we incorrectly believe that if we leave them there we won't be affected by them.

Although at times we may unconsciously define ourselves as powerless, the truth is, our power is only repressed. Repressing power, or holding it in the unconscious, does not make it disappear from our lives as we might assume. Power held in the unconscious doesn't just stay in some corner of the mind to be recalled at a later date and in the same intensity in which it was first filed away. It is transformed, influenced by life experiences and shaped by the effects of denial. Altered and more intense, power is expressed through various emotional disguises. Since this process occurs primarily in the unconscious mind, we are rarely aware that we have made a decision to repress our power.

Feelings and memories that are held in the unconscious, or in the body, are held there by force. This force transforms these feelings, often intensifying or distorting them. It is not hard to imagine what can happen to a strong emotion, such as personal power and control, if it is subjected to an intensifying pressure for a period of time. It gets stronger, more harsh, and more extreme. Usually, when the feeling is finally released, the intensity is dangerously strong.

Repressed power becomes mismanaged power. In most cases, people in the Victim Trap do not consciously intend to misuse personal power. Rather, we try to overcome past pain and protect ourselves from having to suffer from similar abuse in the future. This effort is actually intended to be a positive one, since everyone needs to heal from the past and create safety for themselves in the present and future. The problem lies not in the motivation for protection, but in the way we try to accomplish this goal.

Sadly, once we repress and therefore misuse our power, we do exactly what will hinder our healing and put ourselves in more danger in the future. Rather than embrace our personal power and channel this energy in effective ways, we can become obsessed with the past. By going over a victimizing event repeatedly in our minds or telling our stories over and over without resolution, we create the illusion that we are somehow doing something to protect ourselves from future suffering. Unfortunately, rather than resolve past abuse, we relive it. We are not freed but more

17

indelibly bonded to the hurt, unconsciously seeing the past as proof of our powerlessness. Going round and round and round, sometimes even in therapy or support groups,we feel that our personal happiness or safety is decided, not by us, but by others who are more powerful than we are.

The people who hurt us today are not the first to do so. Responding to them as if they were cuts us off from the deeper meaning of our suffering. Too often, people in the present are merely stand-ins for more significant people from the past. To get beyond our pain to our personal power, we must have a solid understanding of where our pain is coming from and what it is we actually feel.

We need to wrestle with the pain in our past to give us every advantage over the pain of the present. The more we understand why we feel the way we do, the better able we are to finish our business from the past and free up our emotional energy to work on the concerns we have before us now.

FALLING INTO THE VICTIM TRAP
BY VIEWING SOMEONE ELSE AS POWERLESS

Pain and power can be faced and managed, but this doesn't happen in a vacuum. Relationships with others hurt us and help us. While people develop the belief they are powerless through negative responses from others, it is through positive relationships with others that this belief can be changed.

Perhaps you are eager to participate in a good relationship, but instead you find yourself caught in a frustrating dynamic with someone who appears to be powerless. Because people who operate out of a sense of personal powerlessness can appear excessively vulnerable or in extreme pain, it is easy to underestimate their capacity to cause pain for anyone else. Most people who get injured by the Victim Trap don't even know they have stepped into it. If you are in a difficult or frustrating relationship right now, and you have the growing suspicion that the other person believes he or she is powerless over circumstances and life, then you may already be in the trap. How can you tell? The answer will be found through exploring your own feelings and honestly facing the characteristics of the relationship.

First, *notice how power is negotiated.* Sharing power and accepting differences—the very skills we need to negotiate change in healthy relationships—become sources of danger in the Victim Trap. The more you try to make decisions mutually and set personal boundaries, the more you will be perceived as a threat. As long as you continue to agree that the other person is powerless, the Victim Trap "works." But if you begin to treat the "powerless" person as powerful— able to make his or her own decisions and honor boundaries—the relationship may feel dangerous to both of you.

Second, *observe how pain is handled in your relationships.* When we get hurt, the hurt rarely stops with the event that caused it. Human pain doesn't stay frozen in a moment in time but echoes far beyond instances of mistreatment. Unless we regain a sense of our personal power, we carry our pain in our minds, our bodies, and in the way we treat other people.

Even though people who believe they are powerless do not feel they deserve the pain they suffer, tragically they seem to experience an abundance of pain in their lives. Life doesn't seem fair, but it doesn't seem to matter.

Allen, for example, not only suffered pain in his relationship with Janie, he felt regularly wounded in nearly every relationship he had. He didn't feel that his boss paid him what he was worth, he was continuously being cheated by the stores in which he shopped, and other people had better luck than he did. Life didn't seem fair. Justice was beyond his grasp.

People in the Victim Trap lack the belief that all people have personal power, so they must act in ways to compensate for feeling vulnerable. They spend a huge amount of energy keeping vulnerable feelings out of their conscious awareness, resulting in inauthentic relationships with others and the mismanagement of important emotions.

Third, *watch for the "blame game."* When we are caught in the Victim Trap we can be consumed with assigning blame rather than taking responsibility for our pain. We are driven to identify someone to blame, taking a certain satisfaction in blaming ourselves, or someone else, for the abuse we have suffered. Concretely identifying the "enemy" provides a false sense of security by pinpointing the source of danger in our lives.

Unfortunately, this false sense of security limits our understanding of reality. Once we have assigned blame, we no longer have any motivation to explore a deeper understanding of our suffering. The guilty party has been found; the investigation is done. We are often satisfied with a superficial grasp of the crime as long as an offender can be held culpable.

The blame game can hurt us, sometimes in vicious ways, whether we are the ones blaming or being blamed. People we think are powerless can accuse us of all sorts of cruelty, abuse, neglect, and selfish intent. Sometimes the accusations sink deep into our hearts because, prior to the attack, we were unguarded and trusting. If there is even a hint of truth to these critical decrees, the wounds can go deep. The closer you are to people who operate in the victim mode and the more you care about them, the more likely you are to be hurt.

Fourth, *look at how you deal with control in your relationships.* A lack of awareness of unconscious emotions often results in an excessive need for control. Because people in the victim posture are only aware of their conscious feelings, they sense there is some danger very near to them, but they don't know what it is. This sense of danger is real, but what they don't realize is that it's coming from their own unconscious emotions. People who try to avoid threatening unconscious emotions live with a constant sense of imminent danger, which makes them need to control as much of their lives as possible. By controlling themselves and others, they delude themselves into believing they are protecting themselves from the danger that feels so near. Since the real danger is their unconscious feelings, they never feel safe enough to let down their guard and stop their controlling behavior. Ironically, people caught in the Victim Trap have an excessive need for control that is rooted in their feelings of powerlessness over their own emotions.

Shame over feeling needy makes those in the victim mode feel weak, as if they should just try to be better people. Trying not to appear needy to others, they may work at meeting others' needs instead. Obviously, this does not result in getting many of their own needs met in relationships, so the feeling of having unmet needs intensifies. Some people try even harder to set these feelings aside in hopes of finding satisfaction in caring exclusively for others, which perpetuates the cycle. Others reach a kind of breaking point at which they refuse to continue in the same dysfunctional pattern of behavior that resulted in their victimization in the first place. Feeling they "have had enough," they reach into the recesses of their unconscious to retrieve their sense of personal power. But after several years of having been pushed down into the dark caverns of their unconscious minds, what comes out is not the personal power that was originally repressed there. Now it comes out as revenge.

Fifth, *watch for revenge being mistaken for justice.* People who feel powerless don't believe mutual power is possible in relationships. Instead of seeking the restored balance of power that justice would bring, they seek the human suffering that comes from revenge. This gives them a temporary, but ultimately false, sense of satisfaction that some form of balance has been restored.

Since mutual decision making is impossible in a relationship caught in the Victim Trap, conflict often results in a "win-lose" struggle. Operating out of a fundamental belief in their own powerlessness, some people cannot comfortably express feelings with a sense of legitimate personal power. For too long they have felt unentitled to such displays of strength, and once they decide to act with authority it usually comes out in a painful, injurious way. When the "worm turns," it is usually long after the point when assertive action was needed. To justify acting with any kind of force at all, people who have felt chronically powerless have to wait until the injustice done to them is beyond what anyone else would have tolerated. Because they have waited so long to act on their own behalf, their response is often intense and extreme. Acting to avenge what has now become numerous wrongs, they lose sight of the context of their pain and can find themselves reacting with surprising rage.

Finally, *judge the health of your relationships by paying attention to your own feelings*. If you are in a relationship that is caught in the Victim Trap, a variety of emotions will be triggered that may confuse or overwhelm you. Those who mismanage fear can frighten you. Being in relationship with someone who is mismanaging anger can make you mad as well. It's up to you to recognize what you are feeling and understand the motivations and behaviors of the other person if you are to manage your responses effectively. Otherwise you may become entrenched in the cycle of abuse by feeling powerless, abused, and then enraged.

Having a relationship in the Victim Trap presents you with one of life's fundamental challenges: Will you respond to hurt by becoming hurtful yourself, or will you do the work necessary to regain a sense of your personal power and grow through your suffering?

Remember, those who feel powerless are full of emotions but not able to manage them very well. They desperately need your help but seldom benefit from it. They may be chained to a past that didn't involve you while they live in a present that couldn't involve you more. Trapped people need all your love but not all of *you*. If you intend to free yourself from the Victim Trap, you need to get a handle on the dynamics of victimization, blame, and emotional healing.

As a first step in freeing yourself from the Victim Trap, *take responsibility for yourself*. Taking responsibility involves setting boundaries to keep hurtful people at a safe distance and facing whatever feelings we have as a result of being abused by them. Exerting personal power results in utilizing resources around us and refusing to isolate ourselves with feelings of shame, loneliness, and rejection. Taking responsibility stops abuse rather than perpetuates it, because it draws its power from self-love rather than defensive self-protection. Victims blame others because they see power as existing somewhere outside of themselves. People who take responsibility for their pain can do so because they see power as existing within.

The second step you can take to protect yourself from the Victim Trap is to *ask for help*. If you are caught in the Victim Trap, don't go through this process alone. You will begin to doubt your perspective on reality, and you may not be able to accurately discern if or when you are actually hurting someone else. You will become frustrated, and you may even find yourself wanting your own revenge if you are forced into a win-lose bind. As angry or frustrated as you

23

may become, however, revenge will only get you more tightly caught in the trap. No one can effectively regain a sense of personal power alone. Asking for help, however, can be difficult for us when we are in the trap, because we may have been betrayed or abandoned in the past. We may have lost our belief in others, because no one was there to help us when we needed it. We cannot remain alone in our pain and expect to change. Needing others is not a sign of a weakness; it is a display of power that makes humans the strongest species on earth. Powerful people have powerful relationships, and they know how to manage their emotions to keep their relationships strong. Accountability, responsibility, and forgiveness are the tools that lead to relationships of interdependence and strength. No emotion is too threatening to face if we do not have to face it alone.

A third way to protect yourself is to *redefine your relationships*. Ending a relationship is an illusion; redefining a relationship is a solution. We fall into the Victim Trap when we believe that we have ended the problem if we can effectively deny the pain someone has caused us. Then we believe that if we don't feel the pain, it is over. Just as closing our eyes does not make us disappear, closing out our feelings does not make them disappear. Denial places us in the position of being unaware and even naive, which makes us more vulnerable to victimization in the future. We find ourselves in patterns of abusive relationships because we do not see the connection between the past and the present.

We can also make the mistake of trying to protect ourselves by "getting rid" of a problematic relationship. Even though we may physically distance ourselves from a specific person, if we have neglected to resolve the feelings we have about the relationship or if we continue to feel powerless, we remain tied to this hurtful situation. If you resist discussing a past experience to avoid uncomfortable feelings, you are still living from a position of powerlessness. If you hear yourself say things like, "That happened so long ago, it doesn't bother me now," "I don't see him anymore. It's all in the past," or "Why dig up what's gone and buried?" you may be caught in the Victim Trap. You may so much want the pain to be over that you've manufactured a false sense of security, drawing an imaginary and permeable line between yourself and those who have hurt you. This effort that will not protect you from future risk.

Simply stopping a hurtful relationship is an incomplete solution that leaves us feeling the other person has all the power. Powerless people try to end relationships, powerful people redefine them. Sometimes there are aspects of relationships that need to end. In instances of physical abuse, it is important to be able to yell "Stop!" to make the assailant halt. But this is not the only thing we need to do. Once we achieve this, we must stay vigilant and take immediate action to prevent further abuse. Our responsibility does not end because the attacker has temporarily stopped inflicting pain. We need to protect ourselves, get away, and then redefine the relationship to make ourselves safe.

Redefining the relationship enables us to see that we have the power to set limits, draw boundaries, and make decisions about our safety. Redefining the relationship means that we don't close our eyes; we look more closely at ourselves and others to decide exactly what kind of distance to put between ourselves and danger. In this way we can hold hurtful people accountable for their actions, especially if those who hurt us are Victims. This is much different from pretending we have made all the problems go away.

A major component of redefining relationships is holding hurtful people accountable, not blaming them. Blaming others for our pain reinforces our own sense of powerlessness by attributing excessive power to others while doing

25

nothing to strengthen our own sense of control. We are constantly on the lookout for how we might be hurt again, inextricably tying ourselves to the very people we are trying to extract from our lives. We think about them, scheme about getting even, and obsess on how we can protect ourselves from them, all of which results in making those who have hurt us the most important people in our lives.

Blame is a very different process from holding others accountable, which is comprised of the three steps of accountability:

1. Describe the event or action about which you feel hurt. Be as specific as possible. Avoid vague or blaming statements.

2. Describe the meaning the event or action had for you. Explain how you feel and the consequences you have experienced. Be open to other interpretations and meaning for the event or action.

3. Describe what can be done to make amends and reconcile the relationship. Be open to creative alternatives to accomplish the goal of healing. This is not an opportunity for you to control others or hold them hostage with emotional blackmail.

When we recognize that we are powerful and able to protect ourselves, we can be in control of how close we allow others to come. We can set limits on the amount of time and physical closeness others can have with us. Rather than be the passive recipients of the terms handed to us by others, we can participate in defining the terms of our relationships. We can utilize resources, empower ourselves through our community of support, and refuse to view ourselves as powerless. Being abused is a tragedy, but feeling powerless is a cruel consequence that can be healed.

Redefining relationships requires growth for all involved. Genuine growth in turn requires genuine openness—something we can afford to do if we feel personally powerful. When we are confident in our ability to protect ourselves, developing relationships becomes our goal, rather than self-preservation. No longer needing to hide from potential hurt, we are able to connect with others. Life takes on a quality of excitement, exploration, and gratification. Change is no longer feared, but expected.

Rather than look for simplistic answers to complicated dynamics, we are able to hold onto our own experiences while seeing things from others' perspectives as well. A certain amount of ambiguity is tolerated without confusion resulting. Delving into the deeper meaning of things is possible, as is the change and growth that can follow deeper understanding. We openly acknowledge and rely upon our personal power, recognizing both the impact and limitations of our influence.

Finally, we must learn how to *manage our own emotions*. We can determine what is a safe distance between ourselves and others only by knowing how we really feel about those others. We must do the work of uncovering the feelings buried in our unconscious and in our bodies. Understanding the deeper emotions beneath our surface emotions is crucial to getting free from the Victim Trap. Awareness of the full range of our emotional responses to others in our lives gives us the information we need to hold them accountable. Assessing the real danger means knowing the real emotions behind our responses to others.

Once we've been abused, we never have an easy time trusting others. But we can reclaim our ability to trust others as we reclaim trust in ourselves. Trusting our own emotions provides us with the information we need to assess another's trustworthiness. However, this is no simple task once we have been hurt.

Redefining relationships requires us to face our pain and manage our emotions. Refusing to settle for a superficial understanding of our experiences with others means we refuse to believe we are powerless in relationships and we maintain the responsibility to examine ourselves and others to learn what we need to know to avoid the Victim Trap. As we face our pain, we gain the confidence to manage whatever emotions we have in order to hold others accountable and resolve unfinished business that may come up from the past.

If you are struggling with a relationship within the Victim Trap you will be tested by your emotions as you endeavor to turn your pain into power. Feelings of vulnerability, shame, rejection, and loneliness will find their way into your life, sometimes at the most inopportune times. A relationship within the Victim Trap may make you feel very needed, important, and even adored when things are going well. Don't be fooled by this seduction. You are powerful but not powerful enough to save, fix, control, or make someone else happy. Facing your own emotions includes grappling with the limits of your power as well as reclaiming what personal power is actually yours.

Changing your relationship within the Victim Trap is a difficult journey. Don't travel it alone. Identify those people with whom you can talk honestly. You may need to call on these people as you look at yourself and some of the problem people in your life.

You have the personal power to do business with others in your life. You can face your own pain, manage your emotions, and redefine your relationships. You have already taken the most important step: You have decided you want to grow.

THE TRAP OF MISMANAGED POWER

DOUG FELT TERRIBLE about hitting Luanne, but he did it anyway. He hated how he felt afterwards, but sometimes there just didn't seem to be any other way to control her.

"I work hard all day to give her a good life, and what do I get for it?" he thought to himself. It seemed like he could never be "enough" for his wife. When he felt criticized by Luanne, an argument would develop, mushrooming from yelling to name-calling and, finally, to the inevitable punch. Hitting Luanne seemed to Doug like the only way to stop the insanity.

Often Doug would go for a drive afterwards to cool off. Driving through the neighborhood where they both grew up, he would be reminded of the times he'd spent working on old cars with his buddies or hanging out with Luanne at their favorite coffee shop. But as he'd pass the house where he grew up, Doug was painfully reminded of all the vicious arguments he used to have with his dad. A stern taskmaster, Doug's father didn't believe in complimenting Doug because he thought it would give him a "big head." He was also an advocate of corporal punishment as the most effective tool to teach children how to follow the rules of life. Doug hated those beatings that lasted well into his teenage years, but what he hated most during those remorseful drives late at night was the thought that he had become just like his father. How could this have happened? Maybe Luanne was right; maybe he really was a loser.

RECOGNIZING MISMANAGED POWER

Any relationship can fall into the Victim Trap when at least one of the individuals involved is viewed as powerless. Often one person is seen as the powerful one, while the other plays the powerless role. However, some victim-based relationships take a sense of powerlessness even further, wherein both individuals see themselves as powerless; each looks to the other person to save him or her. Doug and Luanne both saw themselves as victims of past abuse, which they believed had crippled them emotionally and destined them for a life of undue difficulty and failure.

Everyone has personal power in differing degrees, depending upon their emotional, intellectual, social, and spiritual strength. Children have less power, starting off completely dependent upon their caregivers for survival. As their bodies grow, so does their personal power. If, when we were children, we were treated with respect by adults who knew how to manage their own personal power effectively, we had models to teach us how to manage our power positively.

Remember a time when you were a child and one of your parents, a teacher, or someone else you respected praised you. How did you feel? How did you hold your body? How did you breathe? Most of us respond to praise by holding our heads high, smiling, and filling our lungs deeply with air. With our feet solidly on the ground, our shoulders move back in a posture of self-confidence and joy. We fill out our bodies, becoming "bigger" than we were before we were praised.

But if we're not praised or rewarded, loved, or accepted, our bodies respond in the opposite fashion. Our faces look down in sadness, our breath becomes shallow as shoulders sag, limiting space for our lungs to expand. We may rock on our feet or feel slightly off balance. Unconsciously we believe we don't deserve to take up our rightful space in the world, and so our bodies (and spirits and psyches) pull in and become smaller. If our boundaries were violated or our needs ignored, we are more likely to misuse our power as adults or underestimate the negative impact we have on ourselves and others.

This was certainly true for Doug and Luanne, both of whom grew up in families where their personal power was violated. They fell into the Victim Trap by believing themselves to be powerless—Doug felt powerless over his actions and Luanne felt incapable of protecting herself from harm.

Doug unsuccessfully tried to win his father's respect, which left Doug feeling small inside. If his own father could not find a reason to value him, who else could? Doug spent years arguing with his father over anything and everything. It got to the point where if his dad said it was black, Doug insisted it was white. Doug desperately tried to prove himself to his father in each of these arguments but never succeeded. His dad never understood that Doug wasn't trying to win the argument, he was trying to win his father's respect. Feeling powerless in his father's eyes left Doug with something to prove to the world. Consequently, he constantly mismanaged his power in his relationship with Luanne.

Luanne, hoping to escape the alcoholic rages of her mother, married Doug when she was only eighteen. Her father had disappeared when she was only four, leaving her mother with five small children and no means of financial support. Luanne's mother worked long hours serving drinks at a nearby bar, often coming home early in the morning in a foul mood. If the house wasn't exactly the way her mother wanted it, Luanne was dragged from her bed and forced to clean until the sun came up and it was time for her to go to school.

When Doug, a tall, handsome senior, asked Luanne to marry him, he seemed like an answer to her prayers. She walked down the aisle believing that the horrible pain of the past was behind her and that she was marrying a man who would make all her dreams come true. That fantasy lasted only a few short weeks before Doug flew into the first of many rages when she burned his breakfast one morning. Luanne felt trapped in her marriage, believing that her mother and her husband must be right. She really was stupid and couldn't do anything right.

Like Doug and Luanne, when our personal power is violated as children, it is easy to grow up believing that we are personally powerless. Mismanaged power, rather than being a trauma from which we need to recover, can become a way of life.

Mismanaged Power Becomes a Way of Life

As is true of all living beings, we are physiologically created to avoid pain and pursue pleasure. No one comes into this world with an attraction to pain. On the contrary, we do everything in our limited power as infants to avoid painful experiences and seek out the soothing and pleasurable ones. Babies cry when their tummies are empty. They happily nurse when offered their mother's breast. Wet diapers result in fussiness, while dry, soft diapers are welcomed.

As we grow up, life presents us with greater challenges

that we must confront and master to become healthy adults. Although the reward for mastering these challenges is pleasure, self-confidence, and competency, confronting these challenges is rarely easy and can be quite painful. Watch the little girl trying to walk for the first time. She strains to move her legs in some predictable manner, stumbling and falling more often than making any progress. Sometimes she gets bruised when she falls. Other times, she feels the sting of embarrassment as others laugh at her attempts to walk. Eventually she succeeds and beams with pride. For this child to master the challenge of walking, she must first be willing to suffer the pain of failure.

M. Scott Peck begins his classic book on personal and spiritual growth, *The Road Less Traveled,* with the words, "Life is difficult." In clear language, Peck describes how personal power is meant to be used—grappling with the obstacles of life rather than avoiding them. He writes:

> Fearing the pain involved, almost all of us, to a greater or lesser degree, attempt to avoid problems. We procrastinate, hoping they will go away. We ignore them, forget them, pretend they do not exist. We even take drugs to assist us in ignoring them, so that by deadening ourselves to the pain we can forget the problems that cause the pain.[1]

Then he writes perhaps one of the most significant truths about personal growth. Peck says, "This tendency to avoid problems and the emotional suffering inherent in them is the primary basis of all human mental illness."[2] When we put our effort into avoiding the pain of legitimate growth, we experience more pain, not less. This is the paradox of pain. By embracing the legitimate pain of healing, we lessen our pain and break through to growth. But when

33

we misuse our power to avoid the pain of legitimate suffering, we create for ourselves more problems, more addictions, more disappointments, more disturbed relationships, and less self-control.

We get stuck in the Victim Trap by trying to avoid pain. Unfortunately, this always ends in causing more pain for ourselves and others. Doug tried to avoid his feelings of powerlessness by being "too big." He puffed out his chest, standing as tall as he could over Luanne's small frame. Moving close to her face, Doug yelled loudly, in as deep a voice as he could muster. All he accomplished was harming Luanne, threatening his marriage, and making himself vulnerable to assault charges. Luanne acted "too small" in her attempt to avoid pain, a strategy that was equally unsuccessful. She shrunk as small as she could, in an effort to appear invisible. Her voice sounded more like a little girl's than an adult woman's as she tried to calm Doug's fury. Instead of protecting herself and creating a healthy marriage, she unknowingly undermined Doug's self-esteem and placed herself in a life-threatening position.

Every time Doug felt inferior or stuck, he had only one strategy to make the painful feelings go away. He artificially inflated his sense of being powerful by dominating someone else. If Luanne said anything for which he couldn't think of a good reply, he would simply yell "Shut up!" If she said anything that hurt him, he would hurt her even more. If he couldn't get her to stop criticizing him with her words, he would hit her in the mouth. She couldn't keep pointing out his inadequacies if she was crying.

To avoid feeling like a failure as a man and as a husband, he transferred disapproval onto his wife. He thought that making her out to be a failure would make him feel less like one himself. No matter what Luanne did, he let her know she never met his standards. He told her in subtle and overt ways that she didn't dress the way he wanted, she didn't have a sexy enough body, and she didn't cook to his standards. He not only criticized what she did, he disapproved of who she was as a person and as a woman. Although he never admitted it, he frustrated her the same way his father had frustrated him.

Luanne, in step with this Victim-dance, tried to create a sense of safety for herself by devoting herself to making Doug happy. She told herself that if she could cook a good enough dinner and keep a clean enough house, Doug would never have reason to hurt her again. Not realizing that his rage came from inside himself and not from her behavior, her unrealistic hopes of escaping the violence were crushed, along with her fragile self-esteem.

Both Doug and Luanne regularly mismanaged their power. Instead of using their personal power to face the pain in their lives, they misused power to cover up the pain. Doug used physical abuse as a defense against feeling personally powerless. Luanne allowed herself to be beaten, believing that standing up to Doug would put her in even more danger. No matter what form it takes, mismanaged power never produces growth. Rather, mismanaged power perpetuates and escalates a cycle of abuse. When caught in the Victim Trap, we may pout, attack, withdraw, criticize, grow cold, or blaze with rage to cover up the truth with grandiose displays of strength. We try to hide a sense of powerlessness too painful to admit.

Mismanaged Power Violates the Boundaries of Others
When we misuse power, we always hurt other people. While we don't have to hit someone to feel powerful, verbally "striking" others and taking pleasure in the impact of those words can be just as damaging. The grimace, the tears, the rage or sadness we cause by verbally overpowering someone

35

can give us the illusion of being powerful. And in that moment, we feel in control and righteous.

Consider this example. Everyone viewed Rose as a powerful woman. She had graduated from law school and then decided to go into business for a major corporation before marrying Chris. Because they were both such strong-willed people, their marriage was a stormy one that ended after only three years. Their close friends weren't surprised when the end finally came, and no one had an opinion about whose fault it was; it just seemed inevitable. But Rose didn't see it that way.

She was furious with Chris, and she was going to make him pay. She used her legal connections to get the best divorce lawyer in the state, and she was able to get a divorce settlement that resulted in Chris filing bankruptcy within a year. Rose didn't really need the money, but she believed Chris needed to pay for what he had done to her. She felt justified in being the one to carry out his punishment.

Rose hurt Chris and Doug hurt Luanne by acting "too big." Doug's history of being belittled by his father left him with the conviction that no one would ever treat him that way again. When he suffered some of those same feelings with Luanne, Doug felt justified in stopping her from making him feel that way, even if he had to get physical to do it. In his heart, Doug was never sorry for stopping Luanne, he was only sorry for the way he did it.

No matter how justified we may feel at the moment we "let someone else have it," when we misuse power by pretending to be "bigger," we are never in the right. At the same time, acting "too small" is a violation of others' boundaries as well, because it places an excessive demand upon others to meet our needs, which is not their responsibility.

This is the paradox of being caught in the Victim Trap. When we feel victimized by someone else's power, we feel

36

entitled to use our power to victimize others. We often remain blind to the real damage the Victim Trap causes, because we feel justified in our actions. Abuse breeds abuse, hurting people hurt others. This can be hard for us to face, especially if we feel victimized. But no matter who we are or what has been done to us, returning abuse for abuse ensnares us in the Victim Trap. Adrenaline often gives a false sense of validation as our actions feel good to us physically. Friends may say that the other person deserved it. But no one deserves to be violated, no matter what they have done.

Trapped in the Past
We misuse power by alternating between acting too big and too small. Some people spend most of their time acting too big and other people spend most of their time acting too small, although at times, these roles can reverse.

Even though Doug seemed to be the more aggressive of the two, at times he traded places with Luanne with her taking the role of dominant controller. This role-reversing pattern had three stages.

First, Doug unconsciously chose not to face his pain directly and repressed his power. This pain stemmed from feeling neglected by his father when he was a child.

As a boy, Doug devised one futile plan after another to win his dad's acceptance. He practiced relentlessly in athletic activities, he won school officer positions, he devoted himself to making better grades, but nothing seemed to matter. Doug worked very hard for these achievements, but not because he received any pleasure for himself in their accomplishment. His eyes were always on his father, and he was always disappointed. Even though Doug was nearly six feet tall, he was never convinced of his personal power.

The attempt to be "all-powerful" is a false solution. To think one can have all the power is an illusion that covers over feelings of powerlessness and failure that seem too painful to face. In her attempt to explain why she would stay with a man who treated her this way, Luanne would describe Doug as having "too much self-confidence." But in fact Doug lacked self-confidence when he was acting too big. The "overconfident" person actually misuses power to defend against feelings of failure and self-doubt. True self-confidence never leads to controlling others, because it results in a contentment inside that isn't threatened when things don't go the right way. It was precisely when Doug acted too sure of himself that he was the most insecure inside.

Since this strategy never works, Doug's pain did not go away. In fact, it grew. Consequently, he felt frustrated but wasn't sure why. He blamed his pain on Luanne for not keeping the kids quiet or for the mess in the kitchen. Blame did not relieve his pain, which grew and irritated him further. The pressure of his unacknowledged pain kept building and building and building.

Then something, anything, set Doug off and he exploded. His body expanded as he claimed too much power, violating Luanne and striking her physically. This was the second stage of his destructive pattern. At this point Doug could tell that things were out of control, so he responded impulsively to get back that control. Not realizing that he was mismanaging his own emotions, Doug mistakenly believed it was Luanne that must be stopped. If she wouldn't listen to his words, then he felt forced to take action any way he could. He always felt bad afterwards, but in the moment, slapping her in the mouth was the only way to stop her, and to stop that powerless feeling he had inside.

In the third phase of his pattern, Doug, consumed with remorse, usually left for a while. Doug's body deflated as he became a sad, repentant little boy. In this stage, Doug became too small. When he returned home, his apology, sometimes with tears, sounded so convincing. He told Luanne he adored her and could not live without her. He bought her presents and always promised to change. But true change did not happen because Doug had not yet faced the genuine source of his pain: the shame he felt about himself and his childhood. Just as he mismanaged his power by striking Luanne, he now mismanaged it by groveling in front of her. In Doug's mind, his guilt over hitting Luanne served as a kind of penance that made his actions excusable. Because he was sorry that he had hurt her and had apologized, he felt Luanne should forgive him, and they would both try to do better next time. She was wrong, and he was wrong, so didn't that make everything okay now?

Luanne misused her power by participating in this destructive cycle of abuse with her own pattern of powerlessness. Not willing to face her own lack of self-esteem and sense of powerlessness, she gravitated to Doug's overt displays of affection and adoration. She proudly wore the jewelry Doug gave her (always after he'd hit her) and displayed the other gifts to her friends to prove that he loved her. Rather than seeking the genuine love of a healthy man, she craved the adoration of an unhealthy man. Doug's display of worship gave her the illusion of being bigger than life for a short time, making up for the other times of feeling so small.

In Luanne's second stage, she could feel Doug's disapproval, which resonated with her old fear of being inadequate and unlovable. She put all of her power into pleasing Doug, longing for his adoration once again. No effort was too great as she desperately tried to keep his indulging attention.

No matter how she tried, she felt she would do something wrong and he would hurt her. During this third stage when Doug finally lashed out, Luanne felt overpowered and humiliated—feelings familiar from her childhood. Lying on the floor, throbbing in pain, Luanne unconsciously believed she deserved this treatment for failing her husband, just like she believed that her mother was simply disciplining her when she beat her as a child.

Luanne started this cycle over again when Doug returned with flowers, words of adoration, and tears of remorse. Luanne could feel especially powerful when he begged her forgiveness. She felt control over him for a moment, taking a "too big" role in the relationship. She felt virtuous to allow him back in their home. Not understanding genuine forgiveness, she simply excused his behavior, and the cycle continued.

Doug and Luanne illustrate common dynamics of the misuse of power, which can be true of a relationship even if it never comes to physical blows. When we misuse our power, we alternate between feeling too big or too small, violating or being violated, making excuses and being excused, but never making any real change or progress. In an effort to avoid our pain, we repeat our painful choices over and over again, remaining forever trapped in the past.

It's important to note that being stuck does not necessarily mean being stagnant. Instead of recognizing and using power in productive ways, those in the Victim Trap develop elaborate strategies for staying stuck. Because of this flurry of activity, most people who are stuck in the Victim Trap are very active and may even look as if they are making progress. However, a closer examination reveals that these people continually repeat a pattern of dysfunctional and destructive behavior, a pattern of powerlessness.

Mismanaged Power Underestimates the Damage Caused
When any of us misuse his or her power to avoid the inevitable pain of life's challenges, we rarely recognize the full extent of the damage we cause. Believing that power is "out there," we base our identities on a false belief that we are not responsible for our abusive outbursts or for our par-

ticipation in the Victim-based relationships in which we suffer damage.

One of the consequences of living out of a perspective of powerlessness is that we overlook the many ways we contribute to our current disastrous situation. Powerless people cannot see themselves as part of the problem, because they do not attribute that much influence or impact to their behavior. Doug gave his personal power to Luanne by blaming her when he lost his temper and became violent. Luanne felt unable to protect herself from Doug's violent assaults. Because Doug saw Luanne as controlling his pain and Luanne saw Doug as controlling hers, neither of them claimed his or her personal power and broke the cycle. If we believe that other people cause our problems and that it is up to other people to change so these problems are corrected, we live at the mercy of other people's whims.

Adults who feel powerless are forever frozen as little children, limited in alternatives and dependent upon other adults for survival. Those caught in the Victim Trap do not experience a growing sense of personal power along with the growing years. As M. Scott Peck so clearly explains, "When you avoid the legitimate suffering that results from dealing with problems, you also avoid the growth that problems demand from us. It is for this reason that in chronic mental illness you stop growing, you become stuck. And without healing, the human spirit begins to shrivel."[3]

WHAT IS THE FEELING UNDER THE FEELING?

We are driven to mismanage our power primarily by an underlying feeling of failure. We try to push this feeling into our unconscious, but that does not make it disappear. In an attempt to feel "on top," we mismanage power. At least for a moment, we can feel like a success.

41

To manage power effectively, we must develop a healthy view of failure. Here is the paradox of mental and spiritual health: in order to succeed we must be able to fail. The truth is, we all fail. None of us moves through the challenges of growth without making mistakes. Those around us watched us fail this week. As much as we would like to believe otherwise, it is no secret to those observing our life that failure is a part of it.

Accepting failure is painful. This pain is intensified for those raised in families that love conditionally, according to performance. Some children are rejected as failures, through abuse or neglect, regardless of their performance. Facing failure for these individuals can be excruciating, for failure represents rejection and, ultimately, death. For them, abandonment means being cut off from the source of life.

Unconsciously motivated by a fear of abandonment and even death, we may try to avoid acknowledging failure by pretending we are perfect. But pretending to be perfect won't make us perfect. Rather than fight this futile battle, we need to confront the truth—we didn't receive all the love we needed as children and this experience was devastatingly painful. Doug needed to admit that he did not receive what he needed and wanted from his father as a child, instead of continuing to blame himself and take out his fear and shame on his wife. Doug's father's inability to give his son the love he needed was evidence of his father's failure, not Doug's. But like most children, Doug assumed responsibility for his father's actions and believed that his father's rejection was due to his own failure as a son.

Because Doug believed he was a failure as a son, he did in fact become a failure as a husband. This sad child became a cruel man, misusing his power. As the result of one of his explosive outbursts, Luanne ended up in the hospital, and people outside the family found out about the abuse. Doug refused to admit it, claiming that Luanne had fallen. He did not want to acknowledge that he had failed to live up to the expectations of those whose respect he desperately needed.

Doug did not want to think of himself as a wife batterer. Those kinds of men, he said to himself, were pathetic. He was a loving husband and a good provider. Sure, he went a little too far on occasion, but he always apologized for it, which made him different from those other criminals. He refused to acknowledge that he had a problem. Because he already felt like a failure, he couldn't tolerate one more indication of it in his life.

Perhaps one of the hardest things for any of us to acknowledge is that we are not living the lives we always thought we would. As therapists, we often hear people say, "I never expected to find out I was sexually abused," "I never expected to be divorced," or "Getting mugged happens to other people, but not to me."

Regardless of the misfortune, those in the Victim Trap feel like failures when something unpleasant happens. They say things like these to themselves: "I knew that was a bad neighborhood. It's my fault my car was stolen." "I don't want to tell anyone about the rape. People will think I'm dirty and worthless." "I should have seen the layoff coming. Why did I choose this line of work anyway? What's wrong with me?"

When our lives take turns we don't expect, any one of us can feel like a failure. Rather than accept failure as a natural part of life, we may turn to perfectionism. If we're motivated by pride rather than positive self-esteem, we may become willing to do almost anything to avoid admitting defeat; we become obsessed with "looking good."

Oddly enough, some of us defend our powerlessness as a virtue. Elaborate religious, political, and philosophical beliefs have been developed that applaud our powerlessness and trap us in infantile, victim roles. Belief systems as well as interpersonal relationships fall into the Victim Trap by praising those who suffer abuse and refusing to confront those who misuse their power.

For example, Luanne went to her pastor for guidance about how to deal with Doug's abusive behavior. She was told to submit to her husband's authority and, if she did so, Doug would treat her well. Her pastor did not confront Doug in any way, but placed the burden of responsibility for Doug's behavior on Luanne's shoulders.

Perhaps the most entrapping are those beliefs that make no room for legitimate failure. Some people fear letting anyone know what is really going on in their lives and in their homes, feeling at risk of being publicly humiliated and rejected by their religious community. Others live with the anxiety of failing God and being punished or disowned. Confused, they don't believe they really have any power, since all power belongs to God, and yet they behave as if they never make mistakes.

Failing is a part of everyone's life. We fall into the Victim Trap, not when we fail, but when we try to avoid the pain that always accompanies failure. We misuse our power by taking too much responsibility and not enough power, or by avoiding responsibility for what we've done and taking too much power. The key to the management of power is balance—an accurate understanding of the limitations of our own power balanced with a belief in its legitimacy. A healthy acceptance of our failures as well as our responsibility in each situation empowers us to act toward others in a balanced fashion. To master life's challenges, we must be able to acknowledge genuine failures while retaining a sense of self-worth and acceptance from significant people. By embracing the pain of our true failures and learning from our mistakes, we are able to feel "good enough."

HOW TO DEAL WITH MISMANAGED POWER

As you've been reading, you may have identified ways you have fallen into the Victim Trap. First, you might see some of Doug or Luanne in yourself in the way you act "too big" or "too small" in certain situations or relationships.

Or you may have fallen into the trap by relating to people who mismanage their power in similar ways. You need not behave like Luanne or Doug in order to be ensnared in the Victim Trap. Whenever we try to relate to people who feel powerless, and accept their perceptions about themselves and their situations, we will be negatively impacted.

If you are in the trap, no matter how you got there, you are likely to be hurt and are dangerous to others as well. If this danger is underestimated, you may suffer enormous damage as well as unwittingly harm those around you. It is important to learn how to protect yourself from abuse and to take action to escape the Victim Trap.

Make Empowerment a Way of Life

For many of us, a sense of powerlessness becomes habitual. Changing habits, especially deeply ingrained patterns, rarely happens overnight. Commit yourself to acknowledging your personal power in every relationship, especially those in which you've experienced the most pain or loss. Retain your sense of self-control while refusing to take responsibility for anyone else's actions or feelings.

If you see yourself in Doug and Luanne's story, get professional help specially designed to help you deal with the abusive dynamic that holds you hostage. Most communities have social mental health services available to help people who act "too big" and "too small." Use your personal power to face the pain of the past, which will allow you to create the life you want to live in the future.

If you are trying to help someone who is caught in the Victim Trap, you can be confused into thinking you are powerless as well. Many would be intimidated by Doug's violent behavior and feel too small to deal with him. If someone like Doug threatens your safety, take advantage of all the personal, social, and legal power available. If you are the spouse or housemate of such an individual, you may need to move someplace where you are protected. You may want to buy a large dog, put in a home security system, or move to a place with twenty-four-hour security. Restraining orders may be necessary to keep someone at a safe distance. Protecting your personal safety is a priority.

Oddly enough, the biggest challenge you face may come not from the Dougs of the world but from the Luannes. Drawn in by their pain and sense of powerlessness, it is easy to become enmeshed in trying to save someone caught in this dynamic. No matter what you try to do for them, they continue to put themselves in jeopardy. If you buy into either one of these dynamics, you will feel powerless, because no one can really save or control someone else.

Remind yourself constantly that everyone has personal power; even passive people are powerful. Your energy, care, and time will be wasted and you'll probably end up getting hurt in some way if you collude with a belief system or pattern of powerlessness.

Manage Your Power, Face Your Failures
To escape the Victim Trap we must confront our own unresolved issues related to the use and misuse of power. Since no one uses his or her personal power perfectly, we all have weak points in how we respond to emotionally or physically dangerous situations. Facing our strengths and weaknesses honestly will put our attention where it needs to be: on controlling our own behavior rather than getting sidetracked

and outmaneuvered by the behavior of the hurtful people in our lives.

While we all have weak areas, we also have areas of strength. Think about your own life. As you reflect on past interactions with people who mismanage their power, you may find that you are more adept at standing up to the Dougs of the world than you are at escaping the hidden agendas of the Luannes of the world. Or vice versa, you may keep your balance with someone who plays helpless but is secretly exerting enormous pressure on you, while someone who overtly threatens you overwhelms and intimidates you.

Perhaps the most distressing aspect about learning more about our own use of personal power is facing the ways we misuse power. It can upset us to see a little bit of Doug or Luanne in ourselves. As we face our woundedness and failures, however, we remove ourselves from the Victim Trap and move into positions of power—healthy power that is assertive rather than aggressive, healing rather than hurtful.

Doug's journey can be an example to us. Like many, Doug was unwilling to face his problems until he "hit bottom," meaning his life deteriorated until he could no longer ignore his mismanaged power. One night Doug went too far and beat Luanne severely, sending her to the hospital. Her injuries were unmistakably the result of violence and could not be passed off as a fall down the stairs. The police were called and Doug was arrested. The judge sentenced him to a year of probation and mandatory attendance in a domestic violence support group. Convinced this was still all Luanne's fault, Doug begrudgingly chose to attend the men's group rather than wind up in jail.

At first he sat in the group for men who perpetrate domestic violence in stunned silence. He hated being there with all those "criminals." *I'm not like these guys,* he thought to himself. *That judge made a mistake by*

47

ordering me here. Eventually he realized he was exactly like them, and he was right, he hated this kind of guy. He hated himself. But his refusal to admit failure kept him from honestly coming to grips with his self-hatred. He had to accept that he hated the kind of man he had become and that he needed to change before he could be the kind of man he respected. In order for any of us to change, we must join Doug in this place of honesty. Being open to change requires that we first admit we need to change. Then we invite true power into our lives.

Although Doug was confused and unimpressed with the meetings at first, he couldn't help noticing that each time after one of the guys in the group told his "story," he ended by saying "Thank you for letting me share." Doug couldn't get over this. They were publicly humiliating themselves and thankful for the opportunity to do it! This was incredible. These guys couldn't wait to get their turn at spilling their guts in front of each other, and for what? The more tragic the failure story, the more positive a response the group seemed to give. Then it started to sink in. Rather than trying to hide their feelings of powerlessness, these guys admitted their failures to each other in a way that resulted in miracles in their lives. No one gave advice or tried to solve the other guys' problems, but something very powerful took place in the lives of the men who admitted they had failed. Doug finally got it. It was useless, and even damaging, to pretend he was powerful when he felt like a failure. To misuse his power to hide from this fact was destroying his life.

Doug learned something else from his support group: There are different kinds of power. There is power over things, power by intimidation, power over one's self, power among and with others (interpersonal power), and the power of telling the truth. Admitting failure uncovered other sources of power he never knew existed. He found a source of power in the group, in being more honest with himself and others, and eventually, with God. Paradoxically, accepting the limits of our power connects us to a greater ability to manage more power in our lives. The point of power is not to look strong to others but to become stronger *with* them. Power was transformed from a source of intimidation to a means of connection, love, and healing.

Accepting the limits of our power is not the same as embracing powerlessness; it is the beginning of authentic power. Personal power knows its limitations and knows when to seek help from others. In fact, facing our failures and managing our power become the same thing. The Serenity Prayer puts it so well by stating: "God, grant me the serenity to accept the things I cannot change, the courage to change the things I can, and the wisdom to know the difference." Realizing our failure to be all-powerful is the beginning of managing our power and creating safety for ourselves. We no longer have something to hide or defend against, and relationships can be a source of connection and growth rather than a threat.

The paradox of failure is that in the process of acknowledging our mistakes we find the foundation for future successes. We have opportunities that were never available to us when we pretended to have it all together. These include being able to do the following:

- ▶ Accept ourselves honestly.
- ▶ Hold reasonable expectations of others.
- ▶ Talk through and resolve differences with others.
- ▶ Give and receive forgiveness.
- ▶ Give and receive love.
- ▶ Live in our body (not too big or too little).
- ▶ Feel and express the extent and limitations of our personal power.

49

Believing we are all-powerful is one of the lies of the Victim Trap. Embracing our personal power requires knowing our limits as well. The balance between power and failure is a centered self. When we achieve a balance between honestly facing our limitations and maturely managing our power, we find our spiritual center.

Pain can push us off center at any moment, so regaining our balance becomes a skill that is necessary in a life well lived. Centering ourselves involves the management of our emotions, the awareness of how our past affects our present, and the daily setting of boundaries in our relationships. Once we achieve this balance in our lives, we feel free from the need to overpower others, control what cannot be controlled, and act in desperate ways when we are threatened. The truth is, the centered self is not self-centered. We are finally free to use our power to love others.

Learn from the Past, Stay in the Present
To free ourselves from the Victim Trap, we must understand and resolve our past experiences. The important relationships from our past set us up to live out patterns of behavior based on our unfinished business. For example, in the attempt to replace the father she never really knew, Luanne created a fantasy father she believed would make her life better and protect her, first as a child from her mother's outbursts and later, from anything that might threaten her. This fantasy blinded her to the fact that Doug's abusiveness was not an overmanifestation of masculine power but an indication of a lack of it. Luanne needed to come to the awareness that she was creating a picture of Doug that was not accurate, and she was doing it to comfort herself rather than face the pain of taking responsibility for herself.

Luanne never got what she needed from her father, and she married a man just like him. Doug appeared to know what he was doing but in reality was just opinionated. Luanne needed a relationship of mutuality, one with balanced respect between the partners. Coming to this awareness helped her to see how the past was keeping her from seeing the present for what it truly was.

When Luanne landed in a hospital bed with serious injuries, even she could not deny the truth any longer. After Doug started attending the domestic violence support group, she was invited to attend a group for wives. She didn't want to go at first because she still believed it was her fault Doug was "in trouble," but she knew something had to change.

As she attended the women's group, Luanne realized she had tried to protect herself by being too small. Luanne's longing for a strong father figure motivated her to excuse Doug's self-centeredness, which only made things worse. Doug did not need her denial; he needed the truth. Luanne mistakenly believed that if she would just be patient and loving enough, eventually things would change. She heard other women tell their stories and could see that many of the so-called loving things she had done to "make Doug happy" had actually been manipulative ways of trying to control his frightening behavior. Her indirect strategies of dealing with power were, in fact, disguised attempts to get what she wanted without having to take responsibility for her needs, her safety, or herself. She had been told that time heals, but found out it isn't time that heals but honesty.

Through therapy and support groups, Doug and Luanne learned that managing power in the present is possible only through resolving the past. Once Doug and Luanne used their power to courageously look at themselves, instead of at each other, possibilities opened up for constructive change in their marriage. They could never change each other, but they could change themselves. What had once been a cycle of abuse transformed into a spiral of love. As they shared their pain with each other, they felt less like personal failures and more like a team facing challenges. This, in turn, empowered them both to be more honest with themselves, and the cycle of abuse reversed. Their relationship was now spiraling upward, with each painful circumstance an opportunity to confront the past and demonstrate love in the present.

Take Responsibility and Hold Others Accountable

Power is something that flows through our lives in endless amounts. Not a scarce commodity we need to grab and hold onto, power is a dynamic, moving force available to all of us. Having power over others by intimidation or manipulation robs us of a more vital, life-changing force: our authentic personal power.

Unfortunately, most of us wait a long time before facing the truth about how we manage and mismanage power, leaving a trail of hurt people behind us. When we're blinded by our own pain, we have difficulty seeing the hurt we cause others. Fortunately, the consequences of our behavior can serve as signals to us, letting us know we need help. We are best served by paying attention to the little clues before our too big/too small behavior gets us into big trouble.

Take a look at the clues in your life. Do you identify with Doug, even in a small way? Do you deal with frightening situations or feelings by intimidating others? While no physical violence may be involved, do you feel big by yelling, delivering sarcastic remarks, slinging insults, or implying threats?

Or do you see a bit of Luanne in yourself? Do you shy away from confrontation, hoping to avoid pain rather than deal with conflict directly? Do you have tactics to get your way that you hope no one will notice? Are you constantly looking for someone stronger than yourself to save you from your current situation?

If you identify with either of these forms of mismanaged power, you can be certain that other people have been hurt unnecessarily and unfairly by you. Even if you feel justified. *Especially* if you feel justified. Everyone who falls into the Victim Trap, no matter how big or small their behavior, feels justified when they hurt others. We will never be safe from the negative impact of the Victim Trap in our lives, nor will others be safe from our abuse or manipulations until we embrace the expanse and limitations of our personal power.

Taking responsibility for the hurt we've caused others through our misuse of power is not complete merely by admitting our mistakes to ourselves. We must also make amends with those we have harmed or wronged. Sometimes setting things right may involve an apology. Other times, further action is in order, such as paying for the medical or therapy bills resulting from our misconduct, returning stolen items or acknowledging the truth publicly. It is our responsibility to clean up any confusion or trouble our mismanagement of power has caused other people.

After taking responsibility for the impact of our own behavior, the next task is to protect ourselves from the mismanagement of power by others. With someone like Doug, we tend to focus our attention on controlling intimidating behaviors, and with those like Luanne, we can fall into a protective role in which we spin our wheels in frustration. However, instead of taking responsibility for the behavior of others, we need to put energy into holding them responsible for the consequences of their choices. This entails respecting, setting, and enforcing boundaries. Drs. Townsend and Cloud write in their book, *Boundaries*, "Boundaries define us, they define *what is me* and *what*

is not me. A boundary shows me where I end and someone else begins, leading me to a sense of ownership."[4]
While physical boundaries, such as walls and fences, are
easy to see, emotional and relational boundaries can be
difficult to identify. But in order to escape the Victim Trap,
clear boundaries must be set and protected.

A word of caution is in order here. Recognize that your
efforts to set boundaries will not change anyone else.
Rather than welcome the changes you initiate, those in
the trap may view the boundaries you set as accusations
that they have done something wrong. In an attempt to
ward off feelings of failure, the misuse of their power may
intensify. They may retreat into a pseudo-powerful or powerless role—like the abusive husband served with a
restraining order who immediately violates it and beats his
wife anyway, or the woman who can never finish anything
because she cannot commit herself to a course of action.
Some will respond favorably to these new boundaries, but
many will not so be realistic. Setting boundaries is for your
sake and will rarely cause a flash of insight or remorse in
someone else. Only when others decide to grow will anything change in their lives.

First, start by identifying your responsibilities. This can
be difficult if you were raised in a family in which boundaries were blurred or violated on a regular basis. You may
have been blamed for the actions of others, confusing where
your power began and someone else's left off. Children are
often blamed for the hurt they suffer: "You know your father
hates your loud music. Why did you set him off by playing
that junk so loud? It's your fault he knocked you around."
Or maybe the blame sounded like, "If you hadn't pranced
around in those provocative clothes, you wouldn't have been
molested."

When society blames a child for being abused, the child

often internalizes the belief, "I was hurt because I was bad." A child who feels responsible for the abuse may turn that logic around and conclude, "Since I was hurt because I was bad, I can be safe if I am good." Many people who mismanage their fear unconsciously associate safety with goodness. Hoping to avoid further pain, these people have invested enormous energy in being good enough to be safe. Depending on their family, being good may have meant pleasing adults, overachieving in school, keeping family secrets, denying their sexuality, never expressing their true feelings, or cutting themselves off from feeling anything at all. In an effort to protect themselves from further harm, they dedicated themselves to goodness only to be abused again and again and again.

Not only is this line of thinking erroneous, but as long as you believe it you will deal neither with your fear nor the dangerous people in your life effectively. Each time you feel frightened, you'll put your effort into acting good, conforming to distorted expectations, and leaving yourself at risk of further harm. This is especially ineffective if you are trying to please those who mismanage their power. Since these individuals feel powerless, they often try to convince you to feel responsible for their feelings. But all of your most valiant efforts to please, comfort, or protect those in the trap will prove futile and frustrating. This approach isn't effective because there is no actual relationship between your goodness and their sense of safety. In fact, being good can end up meaning giving your power away by letting them control you, which actually increases the likelihood of mistreatment. Hurtful people can use your compliance to invade your space. The strategy of protecting yourself by being good simply doesn't work.

You are responsible for clarifying your boundaries with others and redefining relationships when those boundaries

55

are not respected. It is not your responsibility to make others live up to your standards of what boundaries they should have, but you must use your power to respect and protect your own boundaries.

Second, create boundaries that, if crossed, result in consequences for others. Setting boundaries entails expressing your power while knowing your limitations. Setting boundaries in a healthy, balanced way, however, can be tricky. Used wrongly, boundaries can become yet another weapon with which to hurt people and give ourselves the illusion of power.

To set a healthy boundary, look to see where you and your responsibilities end and draw a line there. For example, in the past Doug felt responsible for making Luanne happy. When he couldn't accomplish this impossible task, his feelings of powerlessness triggered an abusive incident. In his men's group, he saw that Luanne's feelings were her responsibility, not his, so they started seeing a marriage counselor who could help them set better boundaries. If they were at home talking about their feelings, Doug would listen to Luanne express her feelings as long as she took responsibility for them. When he started feeling blamed, however, he'd say, "I need to discuss this with someone who can keep us both safe. Let's table this for our next counseling session." Whenever Luanne began complaining to him about things she wanted him to do or not do to make her happy, Doug used his power to set a limit and resolve the problem in a context that could support constructive communication.

As we learn to set boundaries with others, we recognize the need to set boundaries for ourselves as well. While those who feel powerless are dangerous to us, we must acknowledge at least a little bit of this problem in ourselves. To protect ourselves, we must hold others and ourselves accountable for acting responsibly. Doug set limits on his own behavior, making an agreement to call one of the men in his group whenever he felt like his temper was getting out of control. At first Doug called his friend several times a day. But as he learned to channel his power effectively, the calls grew fewer and farther between.

Similarly, Luanne set boundaries on her own misuse of power. Whenever she realized she had tried to control Doug through shaming, manipulating, or tricking him, she sat him down, looked him in the eye, and apologized to him. She also described how she had misused her power to her women's group. The emotional discomfort of apologizing to Doug and confessing her passive-aggressive actions to the group helped modify her tendency to misuse power. While acting small would probably be her instinctive response to danger throughout her life, Luanne was taking responsibility to set boundaries for herself that both protected her and held her accountable. She was becoming a more empowered and, ultimately, more loving person through setting boundaries.

Enforcing boundaries can be confusing, especially when we're first learning how to properly exercise personal power. Boundary enforcement does not mandate any particular action, that you either hold back or be assertive. At times you may need to be both. Doug confused violence with aggression. He felt righteous indignation toward Luanne for her inappropriate behavior in their marriage and believed he was right in correcting her. Doug failed to understand, however, that aggression is the force meant to protect boundaries, to push back intruders who are violating limits they should not cross. Violence uses aggression to violate the boundaries of someone else. A violent person becomes the intruder, crossing the limits into personal space where he or she does not belong.

For example, as Luanne and Doug began to repair their

relationship, Luanne realized that, while she was not responsible for Doug's mood swings, she needed to change the way she responded to his mismanaged power. With the help of their therapist, they agreed that when he started to express his anger in potentially abusive ways, she would set a boundary by telling Doug that she was not going to attempt to help him control his emotions. Once he raised his voice, she announced that she would not talk with him until he gained self-control and could discuss his angry feelings calmly. Then she would leave the room.

If he followed her, continuing to yell, she would walk to the car and drive to a friend's house, a woman she'd met in her support group. She was to set and enforce her boundary regardless of Doug's frightening behavior.

As we look at how to best protect ourselves from those in our lives who are not taking responsibility for their actions, we must face both our power and the limitations of that power. Embrace your personal power by holding others accountable for their actions and accepting responsibility for your own. Take proper care of yourself by responding to fear realistically and effectively, filling up your space fully without intruding into the space of others. In the face of imminent physical or psychological danger, remove yourself from the situation if possible. Get help from others such as friends, family, a therapist, support group, or law enforcement to maintain your ongoing safety.

PERSONAL REFLECTION

Now, let's make this more personal. Negotiating power is a part of all relationships. Even if you are not in a physically abusive relationship, you still need to be aware of how you give and receive power in your relationships. Consider one or two relationships in which you have power struggles as you consider the following questions:

What does this remind me of? Are you involved in a relationship where you have frequent power struggles? Has a pattern developed in the relationship that is somehow familiar to you? Have you been here before?

It is not uncommon to find ourselves drawn to people who help us work on unfinished business from earlier in our lives. Try to step back from your current relationships and ask yourself the question, "Is this a pattern?" Hooking up with someone who mismanages his or her power can be especially dangerous if this kind of dynamic is familiar to you. If you are not aware of your unconscious reasons for being there, you can get stuck in an abusive relationship and not know how to get out of it.

What feelings am I experiencing now? How do you feel when you're in the presence of this person? It may be hard to identify at first, but if he or she is mismanaging power, that feeling will show up somewhere—sometimes inside of you.

How do you feel about yourself in this relationship? Are you starting to not like who you are when you are around this person? This is a good sign that honest communication is not taking place, and underlying feelings are not being identified.

What feelings are underneath what I am experiencing now? If you are feeling oppressed in this relationship, how do you feel about it? Is it familiar? Are you feeling robbed of your power? Is your self-esteem starting to suffer because of the way you end up feeling on a daily basis?

What is your part in not bringing all of the unconscious feelings out into the open? You may not want to share everything with someone who is mismanaging his power, but it is important for you to know what you are keeping out of your conscious thoughts as well as what you're enabling this person to keep out of his or her thoughts.

How can I best express my feelings to maximize healing and growth? This can be difficult if you are dealing with someone who mismanages his or her power. Simply confronting this person can have dangerous consequences. You may feel resentful or angry, but stating this out of context might not be the most effective way to get your point across. Expressing your feelings, all of them, is important, but you must consider how and when you can do this most effectively.

Someone who mismanages his or her power rarely responds to confrontation by itself. Setting limits and consequences are important, and knowing what it is you want from the relationship must be clear. Confronting someone with your feelings and expecting him or her to change is usually unrealistic. You will probably need a more thorough plan of how to deal with this situation. Don't hesitate to seek wise advice from someone you trust. If there is physical abuse involved, do not try to do this alone. Get help.

How can I hold those who hurt me accountable for their actions? Luanne needed to hold Doug accountable for his abuse of her. That did not mean yelling at him so that he felt like a failure as a husband and groveled for her forgiveness. This approach is as unsuccessful as it is unpleasant. Holding an abusive person accountable does not even have to mean getting angry, although it certainly might. It requires being clear about the hurtful behavior and what is unacceptable about it and outlining how amends can be made. It means describing how the relationship can move forward. What is unacceptable now that needs to change? How can you utilize the resources around you to make this happen?

What is my responsibility in creating this situation? Discovering that you are in a relationship characterized by power imbalances is not your fault, but staying there is. You are not responsible for changing anyone in your life, but you are responsible for creating environments where you can change yourself. That may mean changing the terms of the relationship so you can stay in it, or it may mean leaving it altogether.

How have you contributed to the powerlessness in the relationship? Luanne needed to look at the ways she went back and forth from being too small to too big in the relationship. Feeling like you can get someone who is out of control to change because you love him or her is a tactic that almost never works. Many people have died trying. How can you contribute to the mutual balance of power in the relationship?

What can I learn from this situation? What is it about yourself that you need to learn from this relationship? What is it about other people that you need to know? What are the needs you've been trying to get others to take responsibility for that you need to express in a more honest way? What are the resources in your life you have not taken advantage of but need to make use of now?

If you decide to leave a relationship with someone who mismanages power, make sure you know as much as possible about why you got into it in the first place—not just the obvious reasons but also the unconscious ones. If you don't, it is likely that history will repeat itself.

How am I powerful in this situation? Being around people who mismanage their power can rob you of yours. How have you bought into this lie? What are your strengths that you have been forced to deny to stay in this relationship? Can you feel good about them and find ways to affirm and express them?

Do not fall into the trap of making yourself out to be more powerful than you are because you are no longer willing to be

61

a part of the Victim system. Realistically, what are the strengths you contribute to a relationship? How can you use your power to contribute to intimacy in the future?

How can I redefine the relationship? If this is an ongoing relationship, how can you set boundaries that make it safe for you? What are the terms under which you are willing to be with this person? Are there things you cannot discuss together alone, and are there places you cannot be together alone? What can you do to build trust?

If this is a relationship you need to redefine by no longer spending time alone together, how can you safely make this clear? Do not underestimate the damage people who feel powerless can cause. You will need the help and support of others to make your new behaviors work.

NOTES
1. M. Scott Peck, *The Road Less Traveled: A New Psychology of Love, Traditional Values and Spiritual Growth* (New York: Simon & Schuster, 1978), p. 16.
2. Peck, p. 17.
3. Peck, p. 17.
4. Henry Cloud and John Townsend, *Boundaries: When to Say YES, When to Say NO, To Take Control of Your Life* (Grand Rapids: Zondervan, 1992), p. 29.

3

THE TRAP OF MISMANAGED FEAR

THE WORST DAY OF Danny's life was the day he was served the notice that his ex-wife was taking their children from him. He loved those girls, but Gloria was going to make sure he was never alone with them again.

Danny knew Gloria, and he knew she would rather spend their entire life's savings on lawyers than let him leave her without suffering for it. This vindictive side of her came out whenever anyone frightened her. So far he had tried not to be mean; he just wanted out. He really wanted all this fighting to end.

Thinking back, Danny could remember all those times when Gloria blew her top over something he'd done, or more typically, left undone. He wasn't like her. He didn't make such a big deal over everything like she did. He had grown to hate how she demeaned him for not being more aggressive or, as she put it, for not "being more of a man." The worst time was when she stormed into his office accusing him of having an affair in front of his entire staff. That was humiliating. He just couldn't take living with Gloria anymore. Why did she always think everything was his fault? It just made him sick to think about it.

~

Gloria spends more time in silence than she used to. Sometimes she just sits and watches the girls play in the back yard. The sounds of laughter remind her of the times she used to play as a little girl. But she can't keep from remembering how often her play was interrupted by the yelling of her mother and Ted. She can still feel that rush of fear she used to experience whenever they fought, because she can still hear the sound of Ted, her stepfather, yelling at her mother as if it were yesterday.

Gloria hated to hear her mother cry when Ted yelled. She was glad when he left them and ran off with another woman. Even though it never seemed that good when he was around, her mother cried even more often once he'd left. They had no money, and Gloria's mother seemed unable to cope with the loss.

Gloria vowed to herself that she would never act like her mother. She was not going to let Danny scare her like Ted had intimidated her mother, and she was not going to let him ruin her life. She had given up fifteen years for Danny, the best years of her life, and she was not going to take this divorce lying down.

RECOGNIZING MISMANAGED FEAR

Fear is a powerful feeling. It captures our attention, vibrating through our bodies and calling for an immediate response. Defined in *Webster's Encyclopedic Dictionary* as "a distressing emotion aroused by impending pain, danger, evil, etc., whether real or imagined," fear is our natural response when our sense of personal safety and power are threatened.

64

Without exception, every one of us has been frightened by someone or something. Perhaps the schoolyard bully cornered us at recess, our dad took off his belt to teach us a lesson, an earthquake jarred us awake at night, or our car was stolen from in front of our house. As children or adults, we can be overpowered and frightened by other people or by situations that are beyond our control.

Feeling fear is not necessarily a problem; the problem comes when fear is mismanaged. We mismanage fear in one of two ways: by taking flight and blaming from afar or by fighting a perceived enemy, using blame as a weapon. In either case, we fall into the Victim Trap when we do not see ourselves as powerful people who are temporarily over-powered, but as powerless people who are continually over-powered. Responding from the latter perspective, we often take extreme measures in reaction to our fear. Rather than recognizing that at a specific moment we *experienced* power-lessness, we define ourselves as powerless individuals.

Gloria and Danny both saw themselves as victims of each other's abuse. During the first several years of their marriage things went along fairly peacefully, but once the children started arriving tension mounted between them. Mismanaging their emotions, Gloria and Danny spiraled down into a destructive pattern of fear and intimidation.

Gloria, a "fighter," responded to fear by coming out swinging. Verbally adept and intelligent, she usually won any confrontation. Danny was frightened by his wife's out-bursts and responded as a "flighter." He felt overpowered by her verbal assaults and would rather give in than hear any more abuse.

As their relationship deteriorated, Gloria yelled more and Danny retreated more. He took on an air of superiority, even though he feared all the horrible things she said about him were true. Eventually, he refused to discuss any-

thing with her at all. He punished her by pouting, working long hours at the office, and silently disapproving of her.

The loss of Danny's attention frightened Gloria all the more. She feared Danny would abandon her, leaving her financially destitute like Ted had left her and her mother. Initially, Gloria tried to get Danny's attention by attempting to please him. But since Danny was busy protecting himself, he rarely noticed her attempts at connection. When he didn't immediately respond, she'd erupt in fits of blame, desperately trying to get Danny to fight with her. At least if he were fighting with her, Gloria believed, she was connected to him. But when he withdrew, she was left alone and afraid.

This downward spiral continued as Danny, underestimating how fearful Gloria was, frightened her more by withdrawing further. After years of hurting each other, they both blamed the other for the ending of their marriage. They saw themselves not as equally powerful people who were capable of making needed changes, but as victims of the other.

We all must learn how to manage the emotion of fear in order to create and enjoy safe and nurturing relationships. If you are in a relationship with someone who mismanages fear, it is important to understand how to protect yourself from abuse and to resist mismanaging your own fear. Let's examine what happens when mismanaged fear dominates a relationship.

Mismanaged Fear Becomes a Way of Life
Imagine for a moment that you are walking up to your front door after a delightful meal with a friend. Because you feel safe, your parasympathetic system is "on." This is the part of the nervous system that calms you down and allows normal bodily functions to operate. Blood flows to your internal organs as food is digested, breathing is easy and regulated, and your attention is free to focus on whatever

66

suits your fancy. You can admire the flowers on your front porch or plan how you will enjoy the rest of the evening.

Now imagine that, upon opening the door, someone lunges at you from the shadows. Most likely you will respond immediately and instinctively, either by jumping away from or toward the intruder. Choosing between "flight" or "fight" is so basic to survival that we rarely think about it. It just happens instinctively. You are able to respond so quickly because of the way the nervous system is designed.

The part of your nervous system that responds to threat and stress is called the "autonomic" (or automatic) nervous system. Your autonomic nervous system can be imagined as a two-way switch; when one part is "on," the other part is "off." When you are relaxed, your parasympathetic system is on, but the instant you feel threatened or stressed, your body turns off your parasympathetic and switches to the sympathetic system. You don't need to make any decision—it's automatic. With electric swiftness, your interior chemistry radically alters through the release of several hormones, including adrenaline. You may hold your breath or gasp rapidly for air. Your heart rate increases and blood pressure rises.

To give yourself the ability to run away or stand and fight, your blood changes directions, away from the stomach and intestines and toward the nervous system and skeletal muscles. You stop digesting your last meal and actually start digesting your own tissue and fat, giving your body the most energy at the fastest rate possible. All parts of your body are notified and empowered to respond.

If you use fear's energy to protect yourself effectively by either running to safety or standing your ground, once the danger has passed you will relax and "get back to normal." The parasympathetic system resumes control. The blood travels back into your stomach to finish digesting food, your

67

blood pressure lowers, and your heart rate slows down.

If, however, fear is mismanaged, operating from a "fight" or "flight" posture can become a "normal" way of life. When we live in fear, our bodies are habitually under the control of the sympathetic nervous system. We are unable to properly digest food, so our body tissue becomes the target of digestion. Breathing, heart rate, and blood pressure are perpetually accelerated. Our immune systems, designed to protect us from disease, weaken so that a wide array of illness can result, including gastric ulceration, heart disease, headaches, infections, and cancer. When we mismanage fear, we're in danger, not only from whatever caused us to be afraid in the first place but also from our own bodies, which have been turned into an additional threat to survival.

When we manage our fight or flight response effectively, we are able to deal with our fear in an adaptive manner. This may even save our lives. But if we mismanage fear, serious negative consequences can result.

The Mismanaged Fight Response
The fight response is intended to help us protect our boundaries and to hold accountable those who violate these boundaries. If we lose faith in our personal power, however, we may mismanage the fight response through verbal attack or blame.

Blame is often comprised of three characteristics. First, we blame others by making ill-defined accusations such as "You always let me down," or "I should never have trusted you." Second, we often overstate the negative impact this person has had on us. We might claim, "You've ruined my life!" or "I'll never get over what you've done to me." Third, blame provides little avenue for reconciliation since we declare, "I'll never forgive you for this," or "There's no way to make up for the damage you've caused."

For example, Gloria fought against all of her difficult experiences by finding someone else to blame. She struggled to overcome her childhood abuse and deprivation by blaming her mother for being weak and men for being abusive. She tried to feel more powerful by telling herself she was not helpless like her mother. Instead she saw herself as courageous by not showing any sign of fear. She blamed Danny for their failed marriage, current financial problems, and their arguments about the children. Blinded by her fear, Gloria was unable to assess accurately the impact her own actions had upon herself and those around her. As she mismanaged her fear by habitually blaming, she could not see that she was being damaged in the process.

Blaming others ensnares both men and women in the Victim Trap. Consider these examples:

～

Jim hated his father, especially when he drank. Because his dad couldn't keep a job, Jim had to quit high school and go to work to support his mother and younger sister. Jim knew he was smart, and resented not going to college along with his friends. When his father joined AA and got sober, Jim seemed to hate him all the more. He raged at his father, yelling, "You were such a loser. If I'd had a decent father, I could have made something out of myself."

～

Tanya was furious with her mother who, once again, nagged her about losing weight. "Stop hassling me, Mom! It's all your fault I'm this way. If you had protected me from Uncle Ed when I was a little girl, I wouldn't have all these problems now!"

～

"Don't blame me for not satisfying you sexually!" Charles screamed at his wife. Rather than grapple with the frightening memories he had of being molested by his teenage baby-sitter when he was nine, Charles blamed his sexual problems on women in general and his wife in particular. "If you were woman enough to arouse me, I'd have no trouble performing!"

~

The common theme of blame runs through these examples. Each person was legitimately harmed with undeniably negative consequences. Jim was not able to finish high school and go to college along with his schoolmates. Tanya and Charles were molested as children, the pain expressed through an eating disorder and sexual problems. However, each of these people mismanaged their fight response by blaming others, unwittingly trapping themselves in a powerless, vulnerable role.

Properly managing the fight response involves holding those who hurt us *accountable* for their actions rather than blaming them for our experience. We accomplish this by clearly describing the event and the impact we suffered such as "Your drunkenness robbed me of the chance to graduate from high school," or "Being molested as a child left me feeling empty inside." To make way for healing, a practical means of resolution is also identified. For example, Jim could have accepted his father's financial help to go to college, even though his friends had long since graduated; Tanya could have asked her mother to contribute to the cost of therapy and to support her in joining Overeaters Anonymous; Charles could have confronted the woman who molested him rather than take his fear of impotency out on his wife.

However, Jim, Tanya, and Charles mismanaged their fear by embracing powerlessness. They interpreted their

70

fear as the evidence of a shipwrecked life instead of the consequence of abusive past events. They let fear convince them their efforts to heal would be useless rather than recognizing that their efforts were even more necessary.

Gloria made the same mistake, she was quick to point an accusing finger at everyone but herself, which permitted her to ignore the fears she had about herself. To avoid dealing with her inner sense of powerlessness, which terrified and overwhelmed her, she focused all of her attention on the external world. As long as she could blame her mother for the pain in her childhood and Danny for the disappointments in her adult life, she could avoid taking responsibility for her own feelings. Gloria preferred criticizing her mother's weaknesses or Danny's inadequacies to facing her own weaknesses and inadequacies.

Blaming is an ineffective way to protect ourselves from harm. Not only do we have to deal with genuine losses, we also suffer additional losses perpetuated by our self-imposed helplessness. Consequently, we unwittingly give others more power over us than was originally taken. We lose faith in ourselves and in our ability to protect ourselves, getting trapped in a life of fear, day after day, night after night. Even when we cover over our fear by acting strong and self-righteous, as Gloria did, we are actually overwhelmed by a sense of helplessness, despair, and regret.

The Mismanaged Flight Response

Have you ever watched skilled martial arts masters compete? Many of the martial arts philosophies are not rooted in "fighting" as we typically think of it but in stepping back out of the way and then using the attacker's weight and energy against him or her. When someone trained in this technique backs away from an opponent, it is never an act of powerlessness but a skillful use of power. Knowing when to back off and when to step forward is the most effective way to manage the fight and flight impulses, using both together to create safety.

Getting out of harm's way can be a very effective and appropriate strategy for dealing with danger. However, if our impulse for flight is based on a sense of powerlessness rather than on a powerful and legitimate response to threat, we can actually put ourselves in more danger. Mismanaging the flight response to fear by running away from danger instead of to a safe place can cause us to stumble into even more trouble, as it was in Danny's case. Danny mismanaged the flight response by withdrawing from Gloria. Shutting out Gloria's blaming voice gave Danny the illusion that the problem had gone away. Danny first retreated into silent disapproval, then into the garage, the office, and finally into an apartment of his own. Gloria shattered Danny's retreat by screaming at him over the phone, complaining to him when he picked up the kids for a weekend visit, or by taking him back to court for more child support.

Danny knew he was afraid, even though he rarely admitted it to anyone else. His fears kept him awake at night as he fretted about Gloria, wondering if her criticisms might be true. Like Gloria, Danny also played the blame game, but instead of blaming others, he blamed himself.

Self-blame isn't any more effective in managing fear than blaming others, because it draws attention away from the genuine problem. The question he needed to answer was not "Who's to blame?" but "Who is responsible and how can this be changed?" Like most who mismanage fear, Danny did not know how to take responsibility for himself or change things. Instead of trying to understand what was hidden beneath his fear and developing better ways to cope with danger, Danny repetitively tried to insulate himself in a shield of silence and overwork.

72

Danny appeared to be emotionally distant from Gloria, but he was actually tightly tied to her by his fear that she was right about his failings. He thought, *Maybe I'm not capable of properly providing for my family,* and *Maybe this divorce is all my fault.* Danny's powerless retreat from Gloria did not protect him from her as he had hoped. She lived on in his thoughts like a tape recorder playing over and over the evidence of his inadequacy. Danny was not running toward independence from an intrusive woman, he was running away from feelings about himself that he did not want to face. He was afraid he had failed as a husband, something Gloria had made abundantly clear. This fear kept him stuck and unwilling to invest in a new life for himself. He was unable to let go of the past and too frightened to create a satisfying future.

Tragically, his shield of protection became his prison of isolation. Becoming emotionally distant from his wife and disconnected from himself made it more difficult to seek help for the fears that plagued him the most. "Peace at any price," which is often the goal of a relationship for those who mismanage fear, robs people of the ability to go to those vulnerable places where their fears can be addressed and resolved. Managing fear means risking hurt and believing that you and the relationship are powerful enough to heal those hurts. There is no real love between people without this kind of vulnerability.

Mismanaged Fear Traps Us in the Past
If living in the present is too frightening, fear traps us in the past. This can happen in at least three ways.

First, *we idealize the past so the present can never equal its grandeur.* Danny often fell into this trap. He remembered women he had dated before he met Gloria and wondered what it would be like if he had married one of them instead.

73

He often thought about one woman in particular. They never fought, she was so respectful of him, and Danny regretted breaking up with her. Forgetting that dating is much different than living with someone daily, Danny would think, *What a fool I was for letting such a great woman get away! Instead, I ruined my life by marrying Gloria.*

Second, *fear also traps us in the past when we define ourselves by a past trauma.* The pain of her childhood was the driving force in Gloria's motivation *not* to be a woman who was pushed around by a man, like her mother was. What she didn't realize was that she had become the very thing she hated: a woman who was not free to be intimate with a man. Gloria defined herself by events that took place decades ago, not as a woman who could discover her identity in new relationships today.

Third, *we can be trapped in the past when we refuse to learn new ways of managing our fear.* This is what happened to Danny and Gloria. They each had only one strategy for dealing with their feelings, and neither of them made any effort to find new ways of expression. Danny always ran and Gloria always attacked. They learned these strategies as children and, being stuck in the past, they continued to use these strategies as adults, no matter what it cost them.

Danny was raised by an intrusive, angry mother who overpowered him. As a little boy he felt he had no recourse but to give in or withdraw. Danny didn't realize that, as an adult, he could choose to deal with his fear in other ways. Gloria grew up disgusted with her mother, who cowered before men when they exploded in a tirade. She vowed as a small child to fight back. Even if it meant being yelled at from time to time, she was determined not to let any man get the best of her. So as an adult woman, Gloria had no ability to step out of harm's way. For her, "fleeing" was the same as losing.

74

Individuals like Gloria and Danny put themselves in more danger by using only half of the power available to them. By always running or always fighting, their choices for legitimate self-protection are limited. Since most people learn how to respond to fear in childhood, those who define themselves, consciously or unconsciously, as powerless are often survivors of childhood abuse in which they were frightened but not taught to care for themselves effectively. For such people to break free of the past and move into a safer future they must learn new self-protection skills. We all need to develop both fight and flight skills, gaining the ability to step aside or take a stand as well as the wisdom to know which to choose and when.

Mismanaged Fear Underestimates the Damage Caused
When acting out of a sense of powerlessness, we can do much more harm than we intend or even recognize. Like Danny and Gloria, people can hurt each other terribly while thinking they're simply protecting themselves.

Gloria had no idea how much pain she caused Danny or their children. For Gloria, fighting with Danny gave her the illusion that she was doing something right, something to help correct the problem. She desperately needed to do something when she was afraid, and for Gloria that meant fight back. Gloria was not able to tell whether or not she was actually helping the situation, because the only thing that mattered was not being passive like her mother.

Her aggression seemed justified because of all the ways Danny had hurt and disappointed her. His silence, especially his looks of disapproval, wounded her deeply. She believed that he saw her as inferior to him. It had been a long time since she had any hope that he had kind feelings toward her. Even though at times he would tell her he

75

cared, she honestly didn't believe him. She felt powerless to change him and justified each time she lashed out.

Danny also was blind to the impact of his cruelty. Because he didn't rant and rave, or threaten, he felt he was superior to Gloria and free of any wrongdoing. He prided himself on his "nonviolent" response to her assaults. He felt she had all the power and he was merely protecting himself as best he could. By underestimating his own power and the impact of his rejection, he was unaware of the devastation he caused Gloria and his family.

By repeatedly mismanaging a fight or flight response, we can become dangerous because we feel entitled to defend ourselves with any means available to us. When we believe we are powerless, we are blinded to the power we actually have, unable to see our capacity to injure others. As Bertrand Russell said, "Fear is the main source of superstition, and one of the main sources of cruelty."[1] When a person is afraid and feels powerless, he or she has the capacity to be very cruel, indeed.

While we feel justified in our response, others come to fear us, and rightfully so. Fearful people can be the meanest people alive. History shows this. Out of fear, the Nazis murdered millions of Jews they believed were a threat. Out of fear, African Americans have been discriminated against, terrorized, and killed. As crime escalates in our inner cities, more and more Americans respond to their fear by retaliating. Consequently, more and more Americans are dying by each others' hands. As a nation, we are losing sight of the harm perpetuated when fear is mismanaged. In this state of mind, any one of us can forget that two wrongs do not make a right, and abusing others who have been hurtful does not "even the score." Rather, when we fall into the Victim Trap, we simply add more abuse, more pain, more needless suffering to the world.

76

WHY DO WE MISMANAGE OUR FEAR?

To protect ourselves from the dangers of mismanaged fear, it is important to understand that there are unseen, unconscious forces at work in the emotions of anyone who has fallen into the Victim Trap. Many of the things we do, the emotions we feel, and the ways we interpret experiences are influenced by what is stored in our unconscious. While on the surface we may feel fear, underneath we may harbor additional feelings that intensify our reactions. For instance, consider the following examples:

~

Barb had been very impressed with Sue, her new supervisor, when they first met. But when Sue asked her to come into her office for a special meeting, Barb's stomach turned over in fear. "I'll bet she's mad at me, and I haven't done anything wrong! Why does this always happen to me?" Before Sue could tell her the purpose of the meeting, Barb stomped into Sue's office, her chin out, hands clenched, ready for a fight.

~

"Well, what did you think of Darleen?" Sandi asked her brother, Lyle, after their first date. Lyle had been knocked off his feet by the tall brunette beauty his sister had introduced to him. But instead of feeling confident and excited, he felt a cold sweat of fear. What if he admitted to Sandi he liked her and then Darleen told his sister she thought he was a jerk? What if he started to care about Darleen and then she dumped him just like his last girlfriend? Lyle cleared his throat. "Oh, she was okay," he told Sandi. "I may ask her out again, but she's not really my type."

~

Like Barb and Lyle, people who mismanage fear often over-react to situations in ways that make little sense to everyone else. They do this because they are reacting to unconscious thoughts and feelings. We may get clues as to what is in their unconscious, but it is often difficult to know exactly what memories, feelings, and needs are being held there. Often it takes a great deal of effort to bring unconscious memories, feelings, and motivations to light, an effort few people ensnared in the Victim Trap are willing to expend.

To understand how we mismanage fear, we need to ask ourselves, "What is the feeling under the feeling?" Any feeling could be underneath the emotion of fear, but often underneath fear are the feelings of vulnerability and the longing for intimacy.

We often struggle with fear when we are unconsciously feeling vulnerable. Unfortunately, rather than exploring why feeling vulnerable scares us, we often try to cover up our vulnerability as quickly as possible. Consequently, we mis-understand the important role vulnerability is meant to play in our lives.

Beginning in the womb, we mature based upon our vul-nerable relationship with those who care for us. After birth, we are physically and emotionally dependent upon others for our well-being, and it is through our connection to oth-ers that we grow. We need this profound human connec-tion throughout life, not just when we are babies. Our relationships with others are central to our development at every age. Even as adults, we need connection to others in order to be genuine and authentic human beings. In this state of healthy connection, we feel most understood and express our deepest longings.

In fact, it is only when we are connected to others and ourselves that we grow, and we grow only when we are vul-nerable. Satisfying intimacy is possible only when people are vulnerable with each other. Rather than to be avoided, vulnerability must be embraced to make intimacy possible. However, healthy vulnerability can only be experienced from a position of personal power.

This is the good news and the bad news. The good news is that relationships offer rich opportunities to grow and to become all we were meant to be. Life-changing love is created by two people who feel safe, respected, and individually powerful. We believe that both mental health and psychological problems develop in relationships with others. Personalities are shaped by the way we perceive that others have treated us. We all depend upon each other for our psychological well-being. Through vulnerability to others, we can become healthy and strong individuals, capable of loving and enjoying life to the fullest.

The bad news is that vulnerability can also give others opportunity to hurt us. Most people, even if they have not fallen into the Victim Trap, are ambivalent about intimacy because of its potential for harm. Even though we all long for healing and connection, we share a natural fear of the potential damage others can do to us. It can be sobering to realize we must be vulnerable to others to be whole. Trusting others to affect us on such a deep level is asking quite a lot.

Vulnerability can seem too dangerous to people who feel they lack personal power. In an interdependent relationship with another, some feel limited in their power to prevent abuse. Consequently, many have learned to experience fear when feelings of vulnerability arise, and they spend a lifetime avoiding relationships that might stimulate feelings of dependency or vulnerability.

One problem is that we may confuse vulnerability with weakness. To be weak is to be vulnerable and to collapse under the injury by another. We may feel that if we get hurt, it must mean we have no power. But vulnerability is a choice. If it is

79

through vulnerability to others that we gain the strength to tolerate our pain and change our feeling of powerlessness, then we can choose to be vulnerable and gain a sense of strength in spite of the fact that we may get hurt. We fall into the Victim Trap when we believe we cannot tolerate the pain of exposing ourselves to others, so all vulnerability feels like weakness. We don't believe we can respond to our hurts in a powerful way and be supported in the process.

We may also confuse vulnerability with openness. Webster's dictionary defines openness as "not closed or barred at the time; set so as to permit passage through; relatively free of obstructions to sight." But vulnerable is defined as "capable of being wounded or hurt; open to moral attack, criticism, temptation. . . ." People who are open tell us about themselves and others relatively freely. The facts of their lives are available to us all.

Gloria was open but not vulnerable. What she believed about men, the details of her divorce, and the facts about what Danny was doing were all open for discussion. In fact, Gloria was open to talk about anything as long as it didn't put her in a position to be hurt. She was open about the facts of her life but rarely honest about her vulnerable feelings. Gloria's openness was a facade that made her look like something she was not.

This helps explain why people who mismanage fear are attracted to gossip. It provides them with the illusion of intimacy with others. Gloria felt like she had a special connection to her girlfriends as a result of the gossip she shared with them about Danny. But because she was open about the facts (what she called the "truth") rather than vulnerable about herself, she was only connected to them on a superficial level. This false connection does not provide for the kind of relationship that produces growth in people.

Another way we can mismanage fear is by associating

80

vulnerability with exploitation by others, as is often the case when we were used by others to bolster self-esteem. Alice Miller[2] describes these "users" as experiencing someone else's successes as their own, affirming its importance *for them.* Achievements become "co-opted" by these controlling people, as if nothing could have been done without them. They talk about the intelligence, ambition, or good looks of their child, spouse, or friend as if it were some kind of badge of honor they wear for others to see. They treat others like objects, like china dolls or toys that exist for their own pleasure. Compliments are hollow and closeness in the relationship is only for show. No one really feels cared for but typically feels used instead. This form of exploitation is powerfully harmful but hard to identify. Once so abused, we rarely experience vulnerability without fearing exploitation. People raised by self-focused parents like this can grow up to see themselves as powerless; they may also fear genuine intimacy.

It is easy to see why any one of us can become fearful, no longer expecting anyone genuinely to care about us. If we were used and then ignored in the past, we can feel unimportant and doubt our ability to make an impact on the world in the present. If we fall into the Victim Trap, we lose hope in the possibility of love. Tragically, by avoiding healthy vulnerability, we also rob ourselves of healthy intimacy, the kind of relationship that could heal these wounds of the past.

HOW TO DEAL WITH THOSE WHO MISMANAGE FEAR

No one starts out wanting to hurt others. Abuse damages people and their ability to perceive things accurately and to respond in their own best interest. Once having adopted a Victim Trap perspective, a well-meaning but frightened person can unintentionally become extremely dangerous to

81

others, including you. While we encourage you to participate in relationships in an honest and vulnerable way, it is critical that you protect yourself when relating to someone who mismanages fear. If you are vulnerable to those who misuse their power and mismanage their fear, you will most surely suffer the consequences of abuse or neglect.

While it may be appropriate to feel compassion for others, recognizing that they have been exploited and frightened in the past, it is unwise to let your compassion cause you to drop your guard when relating to those who believe they are powerless. Remember, *these individuals experience others as much more powerful than they*. Even if you don't feel all that powerful or see how you could pose a threat, those who mismanage fear assume unconsciously that you are stronger than they are and therefore dangerous.

With an exaggerated need to protect themselves from vulnerability, those who have fallen into the Victim Trap may hurt you out of a misguided attempt at self-defense. Fearful people are especially dangerous because they underestimate their own strength. It's important for your own safety that you do not make the same mistake. Like a trapped animal, this person will instinctively resort to a mismanaged fight or flight response to perceived danger. If you are seen as a threat, whether or not you perceive yourself as such, the consequences of the mismanaged fear response will come your way.

Furthermore, underneath the fear may be an additional motivation coming from an unconscious avoidance of vulnerability. Still longing to be close to others, and perhaps specifically close to you, this person may simultaneously draw you in and reject you. You may feel both sympathetic and frightened, protective and hurt, confused as to whether you should hold and soothe them or run for your life. If you find yourself saying about someone's behavior, "What they are doing makes no sense to me!" then you are probably up against an unconscious motivation that doesn't make conscious sense to them either, no matter how articulately they may defend their actions.

Ordinarily, when you see someone who is frightened, your natural response is to provide protection and comfort. You might hug a crying child who is scared by a thunderstorm, console an anxious friend waiting for the results of a biopsy, or step in front of a family member to defend against a threatening intruder. A crisis, in which someone is overpowered and fearful, calls you to action. You might even risk your life to protect someone you love.

How can you tell the difference between someone who is temporarily in crisis and someone who makes fear a chronic way of life? Making this distinction can be difficult but is necessary for your well-being. It is appropriate to comfort and protect someone in crisis yet crucial that you protect yourself from those who mismanage fear. Consider this scenario:

~

Ben immediately liked Peter, a new associate with his company. Peter had asked to be transferred from another state after a messy divorce. He just wanted to start over with a clean slate, and Ben felt compassion for Peter's struggle.

Ben noticed Peter seemed unsure of himself and had a sad, frightened look in his eyes. Ben described Peter to his wife, Annie, who suggested Ben ask Peter over for dinner. She wanted to check him out to see if he'd be a likely candidate for her single women friends.

Peter acted like a grateful puppy at dinner, confessing how scary it was to move to a new area and know no one. His apartment was void of furniture, he told Annie, and he didn't know his way around town yet. Like Ben, Annie had a soft spot in her heart for this frightened young man, and she promptly adopted him as a project. She spent weekends helping him shop for his furnishings and pointing out how best to navigate the city. Cooking dinner after dinner, Annie introduced him to her single friends and included him in most of their social life.

As the months passed, however, the fear was still in Peter's eyes and he hadn't made one friend, male or female. Instead, Peter became obsessed with Annie. He supplied her with an endless list of problems to solve, all things that somehow required her special help. Annie felt a little anxious but told herself she was overreacting. "He'll settle in soon," she assured herself, ignoring the growing tenseness in her stomach.

Then Peter started leaving little notes on her car windshield and had flowers delivered to her office. Not wanting to cause needless concern for her husband, she failed to mention Peter's behavior to Ben. One day, however, Ben found one of the notes on her car and accused her of having an affair with Peter. What had started out as helping a frightened person in crisis had become a threat to Ben and Annie's marriage.

~

How could Ben and Annie tell at the beginning if Peter was temporarily frightened and needy due to the crisis of divorce, changing jobs, and moving, or if he was chronically frightened and needy because he viewed himself as powerless?

Well, quite honestly, they couldn't have known. Occasionally someone will appear chronically impaired in a way that is easy to spot. But few people introduce themselves with "Hi, I'm Peter. I'm always afraid and have trouble managing my life. If you let me, I'll latch on to you, violate your boundaries, and take advantage of your kindness. And when you try to protect yourself from me, I'll blame you for my pain." Unfortunately, someone who has fallen into the Victim Trap usually looks like anyone else at first meeting. In fact, some of these individuals are especially charming and alluring. Often exuding an indefinable attraction, these people can give us the feeling that we are important and just what they need. If we need to be needed, we can be easy targets to those who are more than happy to take what we have to offer.

It usually takes time to tell the difference between falling into the Victim Trap and helping someone in temporary crisis. Watch for clues. Does the crisis end or go on and on? If the crisis does end, does the person reclaim his or her power and rely less on your care, or does the person replace this crisis with another one so that you will feel forever obligated?

Listen carefully to conversation to discern how this person sees himself or herself. Those who mismanage fear often make their misfortunes the primary focus of conversation. Ask about the past. Was there a time when his or her life was regulated and nurturing, or does this person describe one difficult experience after another? Has he or she ever managed life effectively, or is there a pattern of self-sabotage?

Another way to assess if your relationship has fallen into the Victim Trap is to pay attention to what you feel when you are around others. If they unconsciously feel powerless, you may feel powerless as well. If they mismanage fear, it is likely that you will begin to feel fearful about things as well. Even if there is just a twinge of fear or a hint of anxiety, pay heed to your feelings. Dismissing this signal may prove dangerous to you in the future.

If you recognize that, indeed, you are relating to someone who mismanages his or her fear, start by facing your own fear. None of us would be alive today if we were incapable of feeling fear. Ironically, fear is the friend of life, if managed effectively. Be aware that:

Fear is the natural response to danger. People feel fearful when faced with something potentially dangerous. Fear gets your attention by heightening your awareness and sending you the signal, "Do Not Ignore!" Do not minimize or dismiss your feelings of fear. These feelings are there to warn you of a genuine danger.

Fear is your teacher. To wish for a life without fear is to wish to be a fool. Some lessons you only want to learn once. Thinking of fear as your teacher instead of your enemy changes its purpose in your life. Although uncomfortable in its instruction, it may be a helpful educator in your life. Fear, if managed effectively, keeps you from having to go over the same ground again and again, which is especially wise when you find yourself in the Victim Trap of fear.

Fear is adaptive. When you respond appropriately to fear, you make changes by protecting yourself from injury or by getting out of harm's way. Fear can guide you, helping to prevent you from wandering down dangerous or wasteful detours.

∼

The wisest and most mature people in any society are the ones who have suffered much in life. But the most fearful and bitter people in any society are those who have suffered much too. Learning how to manage the fear in your relationships and maintain the ability to be appropriately vulnerable is the key to developing your personal power and escaping the Victim Traps in your life. Let's examine the important things you need to know about how to do this.

Make Empowerment a Way of Life

If there isn't one simple solution to fear, then how can you expect to deal with it in your life? Rather than talk in terms of solutions, perhaps it is best to use the metaphor of an antidote. An antidote does not eliminate a dangerous substance, rather it neutralizes the negative effect it had before. An antidote causes something to lose its power over you. While there is no one solution to fear, since this emotion is a necessary part of life, there is an antidote. The antidote to fear is courage.

Those who view themselves as powerless don't feel courageous. But the truth is, courage is a quality available to every person. As Emerson said, "A hero is no braver than an ordinary man, but he is brave five minutes longer."[3] Courage is saying yes to life, in spite of its negatives.[4] Courage is faith under fire—choosing to hope when you feel overwhelmed. Simply stated, courage is embracing your personal power in the face of danger.

We can misunderstand courage, thinking it requires the absence of fear. To be fearless in every situation is not courage but foolishness. Managed fear is a part of courage that lets you know an act of bravery is needed. In fact, if you are dealing with someone who mismanages fear and you aren't afraid, you probably are not using courage. It is more likely you are in denial and are in danger of being hurt.

For example, Ben and Annie had a choice to make as their relationship with Peter continued. They could minimize his dependent behavior, telling themselves that Peter would change soon, or they could admit to themselves that Peter had a problem that was hurting them. Pretending that Peter was no threat to their marriage would not have been evidence of courage, but of their denial. Only by facing the truth about Peter's neediness, and their fears about its impact upon their relationship, could Ben and Annie exercise the courage needed to set and protect proper boundaries.

When dealing with someone who mismanages fear, you

need courage to ask for the help and support of others. Courageous people do not gain their strength in isolation. This may sound odd because of all the stories we've been told of heroes going off alone to do battle or courageous men and women standing against the tide of popularity out of principle or necessity. But the courageous do not boldly go where no one has gone before alone. It may look that way, but that is only on the surface.

We learn courage through our relationships with others. Courage is *for* others, or *from* them, or sometimes *because* of them. But true courage is never just about ourselves in isolation. Acting for a cause or value that is greater than themselves, people who have courage also have people in their lives who inspire, support, and facilitate their acts of bravery. Courage causes an individual life to connect to something or someone bigger than itself and become more. This kind of life-affirming act causes an individual to become part of a greater community. True courage results in a freedom to be more connected to others. This is why we tend to honor courage whenever we can. We hold ceremonies, give medals, and build statues to the courageous. Their courage connects them to all of us and adds to our lives. An act of courage may be committed in isolation, but none of us wants it to stay there. It demands to be shared. While courage is seldom motivated by praise from others, it is never motivated by selfishness.

Both Gloria and Danny needed courage. Their problems were not so much with what the other was doing but with themselves. Gloria told herself that it took a lot of courage to file for sole custody of the kids, but that wasn't the case at all. Gloria wasn't acting out of a desire to say yes to life; in reality she was attempting to say no to it. She avoided living in the present by seeking revenge for the past. Gloria rigidly held onto her fears to hide her true feelings about herself, and she needed to cling to an artificial sense of safety no matter what it cost Danny or her children.

If Danny had been able to act with more courage, things might have been different as well. Withdrawing from conflict with Gloria, isolating himself because he was in pain, and blaming Gloria for being "just too difficult" were some of the ways Danny failed to say yes to his life. There is really no back door to intimate relationships. Danny thought that if he could just get out, the pain would be over. But it's never that simple, especially when there are children involved. The only way out is through, and that means having the courage to participate in the difficult conversations, even when you would rather find someplace quiet to hide.

Things might have been very different for Danny and Gloria if they'd had the courage to talk to each other directly about how they felt. Maybe they could have come to some arrangement they would have felt better about, or maybe they could have given each other an opportunity to deal with the situation more directly and openly.

We encourage you to embrace your personal power by acknowledging the fear you are experiencing. Remember, no one has "caused" you to fall into the Victim Trap of fear. Ultimately, you are responsible for your feelings and choices. But interacting with someone who mismanages fear often points a finger at our own mismanaged fear. Like Gloria and Danny, we all need courage to let someone into our feelings. We need people in our lives who can help us understand why we are reacting the way we are to others, especially to those who mismanage fear. While we need courage to let others see the judgmental, critical side of ourselves and hope we will still be accepted, it is exactly this kind of courage that can change our lives.

Embrace your personal power by asking for help to deal with those who mismanage fear. Reach out to someone and tell him or her the truth about how you feel and the danger you fear. Set up a lunch date with a friend, make an appointment with a qualified therapist, join a support group, or call a local hot line. There are many people available to you, right now, who know what it is like to be afraid and are willing to affirm you in your struggle. This is what courage is all about.

Manage Your Fear, Face Your Vulnerability

It is natural to want to "fight fire with fire," or in this case, fight fear with fear. When others frighten you, you may be tempted to intimidate them in return. When threatened by someone mismanaging their fear, you may even feel justified in any action you take. Responding in fear out of a sense of powerlessness, however, ensnares you in the Victim Trap and only puts you in additional danger.

Without the benefit of honest and courageous self-examination, you will naturally deal with fear in whatever manner you developed in childhood. You may have been taught to respond effectively through a variety of coping strategies. Or, like most of us, you may tend to rely heavily on *either* the fight or flight responses, whether or not these have proven to be helpful to you in the past.

How do you usually respond to fear? Do you stand your ground and defend yourself? Do you withdraw or step to the side? Do you pick your fights carefully? Another question to ask yourself is, "How effective is the strategy or strategies I have used in the past?" After fighting or fleeing, do you experience a greater sense of safety or a diminished one? Do you feel more confident or less? Are your relationships strengthened and more supportive or less? Have the ways you have dealt with those who mismanage fear helped protect you or aggravated the problems?

We believe that to manage fear effectively, it's critical

to be adept in both fight and flight responses. If you find that you tend to use one approach more often than the other, we encourage you to learn some new skills. If you are a fighter, it will be important to learn how to pick your battles carefully. Learn how to walk away to deflate a volatile situation. Sometimes silence is the best response if someone is accusing you, blaming you, or acting out threatening behavior.

If you tend to be a flighter, you need to develop assertion skills. You may benefit from self-defense training or from taking a speech class to learn how to speak up. Standing your ground, especially when being blamed for someone else's feelings, can be invaluable in protecting yourself from harm. With the proper support, even the most timid of us can speak the truth and defend our space. The more options you have to protect yourself, the safer you will be. Fear, when used to take care of yourself, becomes a friend rather than an emotion to dread.

Manage the fight response. Recognizing yourself as a powerful individual who impacts the lives of those around you is the foundation for managing the fight response. Use the energy available to you through fear to hold others accountable for their actions and to take responsibility for yourself.

Holding others accountable entails setting clear boundaries in your relationships. Trust your fearful feelings and set boundaries that give you a sense of safety and well-being. Enlist the help of others you trust, such as a counselor, special friend, support group, or spiritual adviser. Feeling protected in a geographical location or in a relationship is something everyone needs and must demand. If you experienced abuse or neglect as a child, you may have become accustomed to feeling fear on a regular basis. In fact, some people have never felt safe in their entire lives. It is time for you to manage your fear by insisting on safety for yourself. With the assistance of your support system, you can decide if your boundaries should allow a particular person to come close, such as setting a time limit for face-to-face meetings; keeping the person at a physical distance and limiting contact to phone calls; or even cutting off direct contact altogether.

Sometimes standing up to another person, especially those who are caught in the Victim Trap, can be difficult and intimidating. Your support network can help you prepare for different reactions you may encounter.

If your boundaries are crossed, be specific about the offensive behavior. (Exactly what frightened you?) Second, clearly delineate the meaning this behavior had for you. (How have you been hurt?) Last, explain what steps could be taken to make amends. (How can this relationship be restored?) Holding someone accountable involves taking abusive behavior seriously and protecting yourself from future misuse.

Be careful not to play the "blame game." Don't blame others and don't accept blame from them. This can be a challenge since we live in a society bent on blaming someone, anyone, for everything that goes wrong. Blaming gets you nowhere. In fact, blaming undermines your personal power and self confidence, putting you in further jeopardy.

While it's important not to blame others, it is also critical to resist the temptation to make excuses for those who hurt you. Stop thinking up excuses for why your spouse drinks excessively or why your younger sister has the right to feel sorry for herself and get you to pay her rent. Don't go along with feeling obligated to make up for everything your boyfriend or girlfriend never got as a child. Stop minimizing the hurt you feel when your spouse withdraws from you sexually because of childhood molestation. Be clear about your experience and refuse to accept or assign blame.

Along with holding others accountable, managing the fight response involves holding ourselves responsible for our actions as well. If you feel powerless, you will underestimate the consequences of your choices, especially if they're fueled by the commanding emotion of fear. Being fearful does not, in itself, justify whatever actions you take. On the contrary, no matter what you feel or how strong the emotion, you are always responsible for your behavior.

The largest grass-roots organization in the world that addresses this problem is Alcoholics Anonymous. In spite of whatever philosophical differences one might have with AA, it remains the most effective program we have for the treatment of addictive problems. We believe one major reason for AA's success is its emphasis on making amends. The heart of the Twelve Steps has to do with honestly looking at our motives and negative impact upon others, and then asking for forgiveness for whatever harm we have caused. It is about taking responsibility for ourselves, not for anyone else.

If you realize that you have overstepped someone else's boundaries, use your personal power to acknowledge your error and make amends. Be specific about what you have done, how your actions have been harmful, and set things right to the best of your ability. Those caught in the Victim Trap may not be able to set things right with you. But some will be thrilled to restore your relationship and move to a deeper level of intimacy.

While it is beyond your power to change others in your life, you can set an example of personal power so that they can see a better way of dealing with fear. By taking responsibility for your own actions and holding others accountable for theirs, you treat these individuals with respect—as people with personal power. This gives them an opportunity to experience healing and to embrace their personal power in a new way.

93

Manage the flight response. If you're crossing the street and a speeding truck runs the light, the best use of your fear is to get out of the way! No need to stand your ground. If you do, you'll lose. Getting out of the way can be an effective and legitimate strategy. In some cases, it is the only strategy that will work.

As with the fight response, it is important to insist on safety for yourself and for those around you. Removing yourself from a dangerous location or relationship can be the wisest way to manage fear. Consider these examples:

∽

Jerry pulled into the restaurant parking lot, dreaming of linguini for dinner. As he slowed down, he noticed a group of five or six young men striding across the lot in his direction. His heart leaped into his throat as he sensed they intended to assault him and take his car once he parked. Pressing his foot on the gas, Jerry sped out of the lot while the young men ran after him. His heart didn't stop pounding until he was a good ten blocks away.

∽

From the looks of the study, Claire surmised that her roommate was angry again and about to explode. Papers were strewn everywhere, a chair was overturned, and music was blasting from the stereo. Remembering the cruel words her roommate screamed at her the last time she tried to calm her down, a shiver of fear went down Claire's spine. "No need to talk to her when she's in this kind of mood," Claire said to herself as she walked back out the front door. "It would be a good time to drop in on a friend," she told herself as she drove away.

∽

Linda loved country western dancing so much that she often went to a local club alone. She knew most of the people who worked there, so she felt safe. One night a good-looking guy asked her to dance and, at first, she enjoyed his "take charge" style. But when she didn't respond just the way he wanted, he gripped her arms. Wriggling one arm free, she waved at one of the bouncers, who quickly came over to see what she needed. As soon as her dance partner released his grip, Linda disappeared into the crowd and asked another employee to walk her to her car.

~

In these cases, getting out of harm's way was effective in dealing with the danger. But what is the difference between using "flight" effectively and simply running away? The answer lies in how you manage your personal power.

Ask yourself what motivates you to choose a flight response to danger. Is it to properly handle the situation with the least amount of damage to all concerned? Or is it to avoid your legitimate responsibility? What kind of relationship do you have with the person who frightens you? Is this person a stranger or someone with whom you have an ongoing relationship? In general, it is easier to manage a "flight" response with those with whom you have ongoing contact.

Often when a flight response is used to initially deal with fear, it is appropriate to follow up with a fight response. Since human interaction is complex, there will be situations best handled by using a combined fight-flight response. Jerry, in the previous example, may choose to call the police about the incident. Once Claire's roommate calmed down, Claire could insist they go to a counselor to discuss how to handle the verbal abuse. Linda could decide it wasn't as safe as she'd thought to go out dancing alone and make arrangements for friends to go with her in the future. To embrace your personal power, it may be important to assert yourself as well as remove yourself from harm. If you rely on flight alone to deal with fear, you may end up feeling powerless.

Another way flight can be an effective strategy is through carefully picking which battles you intend to fight. In a given day, a number of people may do things that frighten you. Someone on the street may act menacing, a coworker may threaten your job security, a speeding driver may nearly hit you on the freeway, your teenage son may enjoy jumping out of the closet when you get home just to hear you scream. Some of these situations are worth confronting, some are not. Some are best handled by walking (or driving) away and allowing your fear to direct you to safety. There simply isn't one best way to handle a dangerous situation. Which should you do, get out of harm's way or attack? What is the "right" way to avoid the Victim Trap when you are afraid?

There are no easy answers to effectively managing your fear. In some situations it is better to walk away. In others you are best protected by taking a stand. No one response is the correct response in every situation. In fact, you might be confronted twice with the same danger and effectively protect yourself one time by fighting and the second time by fleeing. Regardless of the strategy you use, test its effectiveness by asking this question: Have you protected yourself without doing unnecessary damage to anyone else? Have you avoided the trap?

PERSONAL REFLECTION

Consider the following questions as an exercise in applying what you have learned about fear and vulnerability.

Think about a recent circumstance in which fear has played a major role for you. As you answer the questions, think back to the person or event that was instrumental in creating the fear in your life and try to sort out what it has meant for you.

What does this remind me of? Fear never forgets. It hides, disguises, or blocks things out, but it never really forgets. When you experience intense fear in the present, it is good to ask yourself if it could be connected to anything in the past. Some people resist thinking about past events that made them fearful because they believe it will only make things worse for them. Unfortunately, this can result in developing a fear of your fears that makes it even more difficult to deal with your daily life. Being afraid to talk about the things that make you afraid robs you of a sense of competence to manage your emotions. Those who mismanage their fear can then frighten you and undermine your sense of personal power. In most cases, the fear of fear is much more debilitating than whatever it is you were afraid of in the first place.

What feelings am I experiencing now? If there is some connection to the past, or to the unconscious, you can only get there by listening to what you are feeling now. Start with your conscious feelings and try to name them. This is an exercise you could benefit from several times a day. From time to time simply ask yourself, "What am I feeling right now?" You don't have to stop what you're doing, and no one even has to know. The important thing is that you will know a little more about your past experience if you pay attention to your feelings.

Sometimes it is a good idea to keep a journal of your feelings at the end of each day. Many people find this is a good time to reflect on the events of the day as openly and non-judgmentally as possible. This kind of journal is not so much

97

about chronicling daily events as it is about taking note of how you felt about them. Through practice, you can develop the ability to identify your feelings with greater skill than you have now. Paying attention to your emotions does not make you more controlled by them but actually makes you better able to manage them because you are more familiar with how they affect you. The more knowledge you have about your emotional life, the more powerfully you can live it.

What feelings are underneath what I am experiencing now? This is harder. A major theme in our work of helping people turn their pain into power is making the unconscious conscious. This cannot be done completely on your own, but you can start the process by looking for associations to your conscious feelings that may lead you to discoveries in your unconscious. This means that once you have identified how you feel, ask yourself what else you might be feeling as well. When you're feeling afraid, ask yourself what feelings of vulnerability might be connected to it. What are the dangers involved in being more vulnerable? Getting underneath your surface feelings may not be easy, but it is not impossible.

How can I best express my feelings to maximize healing and growth? If you are aware of your fear, you have made an important first step. However, if you've held fear at an unconscious or body level, then you have some work to do to bring it to a place where you can consciously express it. Articulating your fear is important in order to learn what it has to teach you. Whatever dangers are causing fear in your life can only be faced if you can identify the root of your fear. You may need some assistance in learning how to articulate your fears or creating a safe enough place to explore them. Choose your confidants wisely, and try to create a spot in your emotional life where you can better identify and express your fears.

How can I hold those who hurt me accountable for their actions? If you are afraid, you probably want to blame someone for it. But remember, blame reinforces your feelings of powerlessness and entraps you in the Victim belief system. Conversely, holding hurtful people accountable affirms your powerfulness. Learning how to set limits, assertively expressing your feelings, protecting your personal boundaries, and becoming comfortable saying no to others without feeling guilty are ways to hold others accountable. Abuse must stop, and you do not have to perpetuate feelings of victimization to accomplish it.

What is my responsibility in creating this situation? This is not the same question as "How am I at fault?" Self-blame is no more helpful than looking for someone else to accuse. Assigning blame stops the process of exploration, but identifying responsibility expands it. Separating out your responsibility can help you know what action you need to take and keep you from expecting others to do things for you that will never happen. You must make your own decisions about how vulnerable you are going to be with the different people in your life and take responsibility for your part in facilitating the kind of relationships you need. Others may be there for you, but they cannot know what you need from them unless you let them know. With each person in your life you can decide what level of intimacy (or distance) you would like to have with them, and you can do your part in making that come about. You will not always get what you want, but you can always ask for it.

What can I learn from this situation? This question distinguishes people who feel powerless from those who effectively recover from abuse. Those in the Victim Trap lead constricted lives controlled by fear. Blame and powerless retreat blind them from accurate appraisals of themselves and others, which severely limits what they can learn

from the circumstances in their lives. Rejecting powerlessness means staying open to new knowledge, because knowledge is power. Whatever situation is creating fear in your
life also has something to teach you. Facing your fear allows
you to be vulnerable enough to learn certain truths you
have covered over. Asking yourself what you can learn from
each situation is one of the best attitudes you can develop.
If you are always learning something new, you are always
enhancing your sense of personal power.

How am I powerful in this situation? This question
is intended to help you realize that you are never truly powerless. You may not feel powerful, and it may be difficult for
you to recognize it, but you do have personal power. Gloria
and Danny failed to recognize their power, and it cost them
their marriage. When you are afraid, the underestimation of
your power can cause you to be mean and even vicious at
times. Consider the impact of your actions on others, and do
not assume that your effect on them is always minimal.
When you are afraid, you feel small, but that does not mean
that the impact of your behavior is small. You are a force in
the lives of others whether you recognize it or not, and you
can change things. How have you been underestimating your
power in this situation, and how can you make an impact
that you have been too afraid to acknowledge?

How can I redefine the relationship? Your vulnerability can empower your life. Rather than living with the illusion that you have ended painful relationships, you can
redefine them and maintain your sense of control. Instead
of living with the fear that you might be revictimized by this
person or situation again, take charge of the kind of relationship you want to have by defining the terms of the relationship. How much do you want this person to be involved
in your life? Is this someone with whom you should not be
alone? Is this someone you must have in your life, but you

need to set some limits on where, or how long, you can meet with him or her? How can you create a safe closeness in this relationship?

Sometimes relationships based on fear are in the past and you no longer have any contact with these people. In these instances you need to redefine the relationships you carry with you in your head. The actual person may be out of your life, or not even alive, but you still maintain a relationship with them mentally. You must still do the work of redefining these relationships so that you do not feel powerless. Examining relationships from the past is an important part of redefining your current boundaries so that you can free yourself from the Victim Trap.

NOTES
1. Bertrand Russell, *An Outline of Intellectual Rubbish* (Girard, Kans.: Haldeman-Julias Pub., 1943), p. 26.
2. Alice Miller, *The Drama of the Gifted Child* (New York: Basic Books, 1981).
3. Ralph Waldo Emerson, *Conduct of Life* (Boston: Ticknor and Fields, 1860), p. 17.
4. Paul Tillich *The Courage to Be* (New Haven, Conn.: Yale University Press, 1951).

THE TRAP OF MISMANAGED GUILT

EDWARD WAS DELIGHTED to get the promotion he had been waiting for at work. But he couldn't accept it. In spite of how much his wife, Ann, wanted him to advance in the company, to take this promotion would mean Edward would have to move out of the area. Just thinking about how that would hurt his aging, lonely mother made Edward feel sick. He knew she would never come right out and say it, but his mother would consider his moving away the ultimate act of selfishness. There was no way she could move out of the home she had lived in for forty-six years, and there was no way Edward could leave her there without his support whenever she needed it.

Edward's mother, Doris, had sacrificed everything so that Edward could grow up in a decent neighborhood and get a good education. After Edward's father left them, Doris devoted herself completely to his care. She had been raised to believe that doing the "right thing" was the ultimate value, so she wasn't about to shirk her responsibility even though it was unfairly forced upon her. Edward never forgot all the hours of cooking, cleaning, and trying to make ends meet. Doris religiously believed that others should come first, and that meant she should always come last. Ironically, this resulted in Edward becoming obsessed with his mother's needs since she gave the impression her needs probably didn't matter to anyone anyway. It hurt Edward to see his mother constantly rob herself of any joy in life, and it made him uncomfortable when she claimed that the only thing she wanted was to watch Edward succeed and be happy.

Edward always felt obligated to work hard at things to bring some pleasure into his mother's unhappy life. But try as he might, the best he could do to was to relieve her furrowed brow for a moment or two. If she ever seemed pleased, it didn't last. She seemed to believe it was wrong to feel good about anything.

Edward loved his mother but he hated how it felt to be around her. She insisted on feeling guilty about almost everything, and he felt powerless to do anything about it. He couldn't abandon her by taking the promotion upstate, but staying wouldn't make her happy either. Edward felt controlled by his mother's guilt, and he didn't even think she was aware of being manipulative. Why did she need to spoil her life and his with all this guilt?

RECOGNIZING MISMANAGED GUILT

Guilt is a powerful emotion that is often misunderstood and therefore mismanaged. We experience guilt when we believe we have done something wrong, which brings a sense of remorse. Based in love, guilt motivates us to take responsibility for our actions, make amends to those we have hurt, and restore mutual power in the relationship. Properly managed, guilt helps us mend a broken relationship.

Mismanaged guilt, on the other hand, can become a dangerous force by trapping us under a dark cloud that rains on every relationship that could bring us love. We can fall into the Victim Trap in one of two ways: By using guilt as a means of controlling others or by allowing ourselves to be controlled in an effort to please others. Being on either side of this relationship is a draining and frustrating experience because we are unable to fully control or please others. Understanding how we mismanage guilt in our relationships is the first step toward dealing effectively with this emotion.

Mismanaged Guilt Becomes a Way of Life
If we feel powerless in our relationships, we can constantly fear disapproval or punishment from others. This imbalance of power leads us to avoid criticism to the point of sacrificing our importance and value, which further undermines our sense of personal power. As we feel more and more powerless, we respond less out of love and more out of a fear of rejection. The more we fear rejection, the more likely we are to mismanage our guilt.

Guilt can be a powerful weapon if used against us by someone else. When others mismanage guilt, they may convince us that we have abused, misused, or disappointed them, thereby strongly influencing, if not controlling, our perceptions and behavior. We fall into the Victim Trap when we take responsibility for their unhappiness and attempt to please them to assuage our false sense of guilt.

Ironically, mismanaged guilt gives us a false sense of control over our powerlessness by trying to meet the expectations of others. We pretend that we can make things different by the sheer act of our will. For example, Edward tried to please his mother rather than confront how fearful he was of her rejection. He longed to be in control of her reaction to him so that he would be declared innocent of

105

any wrongdoing. Unconsciously, Edward believed the world would be a fair place if he were in charge.

Unfortunately, our efforts to "make" ourselves and others happy are never sufficient to do the job. No one can totally meet the expectations of others. Those who try merely cover over an underlying fear of rejection by trying to perform for approval, keeping everyone trapped in a cycle of guilt and activity. Relationships in which guilt is mismanaged do not move forward to true forgiveness, resolution, and mutuality.

In an attempt to feel more powerful, we may mismanage our guilt, giving us the illusion that the disapproval we have suffered won't happen again. We can believe that if we feel bad enough, we can create enough motivation in ourselves to make sure we won't fail in the future. This false empowerment eclipses our feelings of powerlessness, making us feel we are able to avoid disappointing others if we just try harder next time.

Doris often fell into this trap, making statements to herself like, "I should have . . ." or "If only I had known I would have . . ." or "Next time I'll be sure to. . . ." Each was designed to make her feel less powerless when her efforts to please others failed. But no matter how hard she tried, Doris could not escape the impact of the defining event of her adult life: her divorce. Since her husband left she felt fundamentally powerless over being abandoned and avoiding the public disgrace of divorce. She lived in continual fear that she would be rejected for failing at her marriage.

Tragically, her fear of rejection motivated her to mismanage her guilt and to try to control Edward throughout his life. Edward became a symbol of her acceptability. "After all," she thought to herself, "I must be a good person if I can raise a good son." Unfortunately, no matter what Edward accomplished, Doris never felt the deep satisfaction she craved. Her fear of rejection originated within, rather than outside, herself. Like Doris, we will be repeatedly disappointed, both in our inability to gain the control we want and feel we deserve and in the reactions of others. Like Doris, we will be repeatedly disappointed if we fall into the trap of believing that trying to control ourselves or others through mismanaged guilt will erase our feelings of powerlessness and our fear of rejection. Only when we confront our inner feelings of powerlessness, rather than hide them under the illusion of control that mismanaged guilt provides, can we find the sense of safety and acceptance we need.

Guilt is the gift that keeps on giving. Being in a relationship with someone who mismanages their guilt gives us the feeling of guilt as well, an emotion that keeps coming back over and over again. This kind of gift never loses its value but actually grows more potent over time.

Mismanaged Guilt Gives a False Sense of Integrity
It is often difficult to recognize people who have fallen into the Victim Trap of mismanaged guilt because they frequently place an extremely high value on integrity. However, because underneath the surface they are motivated by powerlessness and a fear of rejection, these individuals cannot be trusted to act in just or mutually satisfying ways. Obsessed with looking "good," those who mismanage guilt maintain the illusion that they are people of integrity working on a problem, doing the best they can under the circumstances. They hide behind the psychological facade of taking responsibility for some concern they claim is important to them. But the truth is, mismanaged guilt is based on fear, and its ultimate goal is to avoid punishment. Doris secretly felt so guilty about her divorce that she would go to any lengths to win the approval of others. Those like Doris are driven to avoid something rather than accomplish a

107

goal. Masquerading as responsibility, fear-based guilt is actually a disguised form of self-protection. These people are more interested in shielding themselves from the pain of disapproval than in genuinely caring about others. Before they can love and care freely, the underlying issues must be resolved.

To offset her guilt, Doris became the "super mom," serving as den mother for Edward's Boy Scout troop, baking cookies for his classmates, and helping him succeed academically. Rather than assist Edward in growing as a separate individual, however, Doris insisted he succeed in ways that made her look good to others. Whenever he tried to make his own decisions or pursue an activity in which she could not directly participate, Doris would act hurt and withdrawn, saying things to make Edward feel guilty such as, "No, go ahead without me. I don't mind sitting here all by myself." As a boy, Edward often succumbed to these manipulations, but when he did do something without his mother he'd feel like an ungrateful, disappointing son.

As an adult, Edward continued to suffer from his mother's mismanaged guilt and manipulations. Doris called Edward often, visited him several times a week, and always saw him on the weekends. She loved telling her friends at church how devoted Edward was to her. From this flurry of activity, one would guess they had a close relationship. However, even though the mismanagement of guilt can result in a great deal of activity, it rarely results in any intimacy. Doris was busy avoiding self-punishment rather than investing in genuine intimacy with her son. Mismanaged guilt causes us to pretend, blocking us from saying how we really feel, and can even motivate us to lie. Instead of having honest conversations with each other, Doris and Edward would act as if things were "just fine," even though they both were suffering in some way.

Another outcome of mismanaged guilt is perfectionism.

Rather than focusing on doing the right thing, perfectionists are terrified of doing the wrong thing. Doris invested enormous energy into avoiding mistakes—an all-consuming commitment for anyone to have in life. Any criticism caused Doris to doubt herself as a woman. Any mistake threatened to undermine her self-worth. When would she ever have done enough? How could she ever relax? She never felt secure or good about herself, because her next mistake could reveal to everyone that she was the kind of woman who deserved to be left by her husband. There was always something she could have been done better or something she needed to worry about. Everyone around her posed a threat by being able to point out something she had done or left undone that she could feel guilty about.

Without realizing it, Doris transferred this feeling to God. Terrified of making a mistake, Doris had a difficult time making any decision on her own. She believed God wanted her to be a "good person," as well as a good mother and wife. Often consumed with wondering what God wanted her to do, she failed to develop strength of character and self-confidence. She believed either God was doing it for her or Satan was doing it to her, but she never felt personally powerful enough to make responsible decisions in her life. No matter how loving or forgiving God really was, she believed God accepted her based upon her performance. Her security was based either on how good she could be, or how bad she felt if her behavior fell short of perfection.

Since none of us recognizes his or her genuine power or responsibilities when in the Victim Trap, we can fail to protect ourselves from revictimization. As we desperately try to please others because we feel guilty, we often feel humiliated over having our dignity taken away.

Doris believed she was powerless to be any different than she was. To disappoint or displease others was, in her mind, morally wrong and could be punishable by God. In her marriage, pleasing her husband was a survival strategy. She feared that if he was unhappy she would lose him and it would be her fault. Their divorce was a tragic confirmation of this belief. This was a very familiar feeling from her childhood as well. Right behavior determined whether or not she was loved, so she never forgot the rules.

Just because Doris felt excessively guilty does not mean she necessarily took responsibility for her own well-being or actions. True, when we fall into the Victim Trap we may genuinely want things to be made right, but mismanaged guilt distorts our understanding of true responsibility because the motivation is to avoid pain rather than face legitimate suffering inherent in growth and intimacy. We may focus our attention on finding the "correct" behavior in every circumstance, which usually includes trying to control others, hoping to be rewarded with approval and a life without pain.

Based on the belief, "If I am good, I won't suffer," Doris hoped that people would not be disappointed with her as a mother and that she could be happy. People would love her if they approved of her son. Her conscience, guilt-ridden since the divorce, would be satisfied if Edward succeeded. Doris couldn't see that this plan was destined for failure. Because Doris's plan for happiness was rooted in her sense of powerlessness, she could only be happy (and guilt-free) if she were in control of Edward's behavior. Edward, as someone trying to get out of the Victim Trap, was struggling to be his own person and to resist her domination. He didn't want to hurt his mother and, at the same time, he needed to have his own sense of personal power.

A healthy conscience with love as its foundation feels guilt that leads to remorse, apology, and making amends. However, when we're caught in the Victim Trap, we cannot trust our conscience because our guilt feelings are rooted in fear. Edward struggled with the guilt he felt regarding his mother, trying to resist being controlled by her disapproval. Would Edward, like his mother before him, live his life in fear? Rather than follow the dictates of a distorted conscience, would he face his true responsibility to himself and his family?

Ideally, Edward needed his mother to face up to the deception, manipulations, and unhappiness in her life. Her genuine responsibility was to offer Edward an honest relationship with an imperfect woman who loved him today. Responsibility based on personal power acknowledges that suffering cannot be avoided, no matter how good we are. What we can do is care.

But what do we do if, as in Edward's situation, we don't get the love and mutuality we need? Resisting manipulative guilt can be very difficult and frightening. Relationships based on guilt may keep people close physically but never emotionally. We are robbed of the motivation to enhance and heal the relationship. When we want approval at all costs we're reluctant to make waves or express feelings that may be considered unacceptable. Edward was physically there for his mother whenever she needed him, but he never felt safe around her or emotionally connected to her. He knew he was important to her, but he never felt treasured by her. He was useful but not valuable.

Because mismanaged guilt takes so much energy to understand and respond to, we can become deficient in our ability to respond to others. Our "response ability" falls short of genuine responsibility because we become more concerned about protecting ourselves than about being truthful, especially if the truth is painful. Without intending to, we can fall into the Victim Trap in our attempt to escape from those who mismanage guilt. Coming to grips with our

111

weaknesses, forgiving ourselves for our failures, and holding others accountable are the signs of true responsibility. This can never be achieved when we are being seduced by fear-based guilt.

The mismanagement of guilt can often be traced back to childhood when guilt was used by caregivers to keep children under their control. In healthy families where the standard of conduct is consistent, children are held accountable for their actions and then given the opportunity to make amends. Adults who mismanage guilt often grew up with parents who disciplined them whenever they did something "wrong" as determined by their parents or other authority figures, thereby teaching them to feel "guilty" whenever authority figures did not like what they had done. Feeling good about themselves by being given an opportunity to do things right and get recognition for it rarely happened. These children were taught to live with a sense of guilt as if this burden were normal or even "godly."

Mismanaged Guilt Traps Victims in the Past
Like all mismanaged feelings, mismanaged guilt attaches us to past abuse and deprivation. Even though it may be our earnest attempt to free ourselves from emotional bondage, mismanaged guilt actually ties us to the very thing from which we are trying to get free.

Often mismanaged guilt keeps us obsessively thinking about the past. We turn events over and over in our minds trying to relive them differently this time. Promises of how we are going to be different in the future are predicated on memories of events we wish had never happened. Doris's obsession with her divorce kept her continually looking back. Her inability to let go of the past served as a major obstacle for Edward to embrace his future. As long as his mother controlled him with guilt, Edward was unable to be emotionally and physically free to move forward.

Like Edward, we may have been "guilt-tripped" by those struggling to break free from a guilt-ridden past. Sometimes we may feel guilty about things we have done or not done, and those actions are used by someone who mismanages guilt to blackmail us emotionally.

A good example of this is Claudia. Claudia grew up in a small midwestern town with her younger sister in a close community of friends and family. When she was eleven, she came upon her sister playing in the woods with an older boy they knew from the area. The boy insisted they weren't doing anything wrong and Claudia should let them continue to "play" for a while alone. Feeling uncomfortable with this, Claudia protested at first, but the boy's insistence became too threatening for her and she backed down. He was older and intimidating, and she did not know what to do. The boy demanded that Claudia never tell anyone about their playing in the woods or he would hurt her and possibly even her sister.

Years later Claudia learned from her sister that she had been sexually molested by this boy. Claudia was overwhelmed with guilt for not having protected her sister from him. Claudia can never forgive herself for that day in the woods and can never imagine not feeling guilty about it. Twenty years later, the injury of the neighbor boy's actions lives on in Claudia's life as if it had happened today.

No amount of penance can satisfy mismanaged guilt. It is a sentence of self-punishment that should be served forever, if necessary. Those of us who mismanage guilt become our own judge and jury for some crime we conclude we have committed and have not yet suffered enough for. Rather than manage her guilt properly by taking responsibility for her actions and making amends with her sister, Claudia blamed herself for all of the boy's, and her sister's, poor choices. Difficulties that came up years later, in seemingly unrelated circumstances, became additional reasons for Claudia to feel guilty about her cowardice. In fact, every time her sister displayed some type of emotional problem, Claudia used it to beat herself up.

Long after her sister had redefined her relationship to her childhood molester, Claudia's guilt kept her entrenched in exactly the same relationship with him as she'd had when she was eleven. Attempting to redo the past, she never left it.

In fact, Claudia clung to her guilt with a vengeance. When her friends comforted her or told her it wasn't her fault, Claudia often became angry. She tried to make her friends feel guilty for their lack of understanding or concern for her sister. Those friends who buckled under Claudia's guilt-laden barrage remained in her life, but those who refused to go along with her soon had no place in her life. Sadly, this can be the "either-or" choice we sometimes have to make with these individuals in our lives.

Other times we have played no part in past pain but feel sorry for the pain someone else has suffered and will do almost anything to make up for the suffering and loss. Stan, a single man in his late twenties, came to counseling because he felt guilty about ending a relationship with Tina, a woman he had dated for over a year. Early in the relationship, Tina told Stan about her difficult childhood and other men who had abandoned her at moments of need. Stan vowed to himself to be different from the other men and to help Tina heal from her past. But no matter what he did, Stan was unable to keep Tina from fearing his rejection.

Even though Stan had been faithful to Tina throughout their relationship, Tina often flew into fits of tearful accusations that Stan was not attentive enough to her. She broke dishes, cried for hours and threatened to kill herself if Stan ever left her. Eventually, the guilt and emotional blackmail was too oppressive and Stan ended their relationship. But Stan still wishes he could have been a "better man and able to give her the love she needed."

Like Claudia and Stan, we can become tied to the guilt of the past because feeling guilty becomes the most familiar emotional state we know. If we don't feel guilty, then we start to feel bad for not taking our responsibilities seriously enough. Feeling guilty about not feeling guilty keeps mismanaged guilt alive. Because certain relationships can never be made right, guilt becomes the "normal" feeling we may experience. To give up feeling guilt about certain people or events would feel too uncomfortable, and these feelings can go on for a lifetime.

Mismanaged Guilt Underestimates the Damage Caused

Mismanaged guilt is selective; it is very sensitive to fear of punishment, but it is not as sensitive to people. Because those who fall into the Victim Trap fear the disapproval of others, they are unable to truly love others, to listen to them, to genuinely respond to their needs. Their ability to work out difficulties with others is constricted because they are afraid of doing yet another thing wrong for which they will feel additional guilt. Edward was initially hurt by the way his mother mismanaged her guilt feelings. He then eventually mismanaged his own guilt and, in turn, victimized others.

As both Doris and Edward allowed themselves to be controlled by the emotion of guilt, their efforts were diverted away from their genuine responsibilities. While Doris was responsible for caring for her son to a certain degree, her obsession with him stole time and energy away from his wife and children. Time after time, Edward disappointed his family in order to respond to the excessive demands of his mother. He missed his son's piano recital because his mother called him at the last minute to come over and fix a broken appliance. Edward couldn't afford to send his daughter to camp one summer, because he'd spent so much money refurnishing his mother's living room.

His wife, Ann, was so wounded by Edward's neglect that she no longer knew if she loved him. She knew she didn't trust him anymore. Who really was the most important woman in his life, anyway? Ann had grown extremely weary of his many excuses. "She's an elderly woman," he'd say. "She has no one in her life and she needs me. What am I supposed to do, abandon her and let her become homeless?" Each time his family expressed pain over Doris's abuse of Edward and his neglect of them, he responded not with understanding or any intention of changing his behavior but with reasons why they should accept this mistreatment.

Like mother, like son, unfortunately. When Edward was especially tired, he would try to control his family with guilt, just like his mother controlled him. "How can you be so selfish?" he'd ask his children. "You're young and strong, and she's all by herself. I expect more from you than this self-centered whining." Secretly he was disappointed that his family didn't admire him for what he was doing. Here he was making all these sacrifices for his mother and being a truly fine, responsible man. "Why can't they see that and give me credit for it instead of complaining all the time?"

Edward's mismanaged guilt about his mother kept him from feeling the kind of guilt about Ann that could have made a positive difference in his life, the kind that is based on love. Feeling guilty for allowing repetitive abuse by others can cause some people to feel all the more entitled to protect themselves at every opportunity in the future. When people mismanage their guilt over having been victimized, they don't feel truly guilty about hurting others. If Edward had acknowledged, rather than denied, his true responsibilities, he could have set aside the false guilt he received from his mother and used his feelings of true guilt to make changes in his life that might have brought him closer to his wife and empowered him to deal constructively with his relationship with his mother. Instead, his fear-based guilt only limited Edward's ability to resolve problems and pulled him further into the Victim Trap.

Edward and Doris jointly participated in the charade. Doris's mismanaged guilt blinded her to the truth about her relationship with Edward. Instead of their relationship giving them energy and nurturance, it actually drained the vitality they both needed. Doris felt bad most of the time, but she never was able to fully grasp why. Her guilt was a false explanation for why she felt so bad. She would often think that the heavy feeling she carried with her was the result of her responsibility to care for her son, as if she was some kind of saint in distress. Likewise, Edward excused her rigidity, negativity, and controlling manner as personality quirks of a good, but elderly, woman who had lived a difficult life. "It's never been easy for her," he would explain to his wife. "We just have to be more understanding." But people who mismanage guilt base their actions on fear and do not really want to be understood. They just want painful feelings to go away.

For some, this attitude of denial extends itself to the physical abuse they feel they must endure from others. Some women stay in abusive relationships as a kind of proof of their superior ability to "love." For some men, to acknowledge that being hit by a woman is abuse is to admit that they are not really "a man." The guilt that causes them to fear the criticism of others poses more of a threat to them than physical harm by a woman. Like Edward, some men prove their strength by their capacity to suffer whatever punishment is directed their way. Unfortunately, when their mismanaged guilt is a primary motivation, nothing ever gets proven. Instead of proving themselves strong, they only avoid being seen as weak. They feel additional guilt for not acting in their own defense but are clueless about how to take better care of themselves. They may hope their guilt will motivate them to conduct themselves differently in the future so that the abuse will never repeat itself. But mismanaging guilt does not protect them from harm, it only makes them more susceptible to the manipulations of others.

When we mismanage our guilt we are satisfied with superficial understandings between people, which limit our ability to talk about things in depth. We seek to make uncomfortable conversations stop as soon as possible, even if the discomfort lives on inside. Motivated to avoid pain rather than understand what is really wrong in our relationships, we mismanage guilt and its origins by seeking solutions that never satisfy.

Like Edward and his mother, we can go to great lengths not to face the negative consequences of our self-deception. Doris could never admit that her guilt was a primary motivation in her relationship with Edward because she believed this would be an admission that she was doing something very wrong, and this would cause Edward not to want to see her anymore. On the other hand, Edward could not admit his true responsibility either, so he was forced to "take" whatever abuse she handed him as some kind of display of how strong their relationship was and how much they really loved each other. He could excuse his mother's abusive behavior, but he could never forgive himself if he turned out to be the same kind of weak man as his father, who ran from his responsibilities because it got too tough for him.

Doris and Edward led tragic lives, negatively impacting all who loved and depended on them. Since we have all been victimized in some fashion, we all risk falling into this same trap of mismanaged guilt and unintentionally passing on

118

this distortion to our children, our spouses, and our friends.

Guilt that is properly managed causes people to want to repair misunderstandings in important relationships and get to a place where they can experience more connection to each other. It does not excuse abusive behavior but motivates people to come to a more profound understanding so that abuse can stop.

WHY DO WE MISMANAGE OUR GUILT?

Mismanaged guilt keeps people from paying attention to the real problems in their lives. If we fall into the Victim Trap, there is one fear that leads us to mismanage guilt more than any other: the fear of rejection. Because we believe we are basically powerless, we live with the constant fear we could lose our place in the hearts of those around us at any time, if we were ever there in the first place. Not believing we are truly loved, we fear rejection and, as a result, behave in ways we hope will guarantee others will love us.

Rejection is one of the greatest fears in anyone's life. No one wants to be left, especially if we are blamed for something we have done. This kind of abandonment leaves psychological scars that last for years, sometimes even a lifetime. Most people will go to great lengths to protect themselves from the experience of rejection. Doris lived her life around this one effort. The fear of rejection motivated her to endure a lifetime of self-sacrifice and humiliation. She had experienced it once in her marriage, and no amount of personal suffering would have been worse than having to go through it again.

Guilt that results from fear of rejection is not always easy to understand. A mother's concern for her son is a good thing, so on the surface it was not always clear why Doris did the things she did. Her motivation for the type of

119

relationship she had with Edward was buried deep below the surface and required some examination to really understand. Was she so concerned about him because she loved him and felt loved by him, or because she feared that if she didn't try to show her concern constantly she would lose his love? Did she encourage his achievements because she wanted the best for him, or because she used his successes to earn acceptance from others?

We always lack honesty when we mismanage our emotions. If we don't want to know the whole truth about how we feel, we won't want others to know either. However, those with whom we are least truthful are typically ourselves. Oddly enough, this lack of honesty serves an unconscious purpose. If our underlying fear of rejection remains hidden from view, maybe it will never come true.

This dynamic is common in extramarital affairs. Alfred, a professor in his forties, told us about his troubled marriage and his despair over not knowing what to do about it. Talking with his wife about their problems usually resulted in a fight that only seemed to make things worse. Too proud to admit he was feeling rejected by the most important woman in his life, he began to take long business lunches with his secretary who "really listened" to him. Feeling the acceptance of an attractive woman, who valued his professional skills and who didn't place the mundane demands on him that his wife and family did, covered over Alfred's feelings of rejection. At first he felt a little guilty about his romantic feelings for his secretary, but soon that got covered over too. Alfred's worst fear, rejection by his wife, became a reality when she learned of the affair and filed for divorce. By refusing to face his fears directly, he unwittingly set himself up for rejection and true moral guilt.

Rejection can be overt or covert. Overt rejection is unmistakable and obvious to all: a mother leaves her child on the doorstep of the police station; a man comes home from work to find his wife has moved out; a woman refuses to accept her friend's phone calls or answer her letters. Rejection can be one of the most painful experiences in life.

Covert rejection can be just as painful, only it is more difficult to identify because the experience of being unwanted comes through indirect acts or obscure conduct that may have more than one meaning. We can feel abandoned yet confused about whether or not we are really being rejected.

An example of the experience of covert rejection comes from parents who overcontrol their children. On the surface they appear to be motivated by a genuine interest in their child's well-being. But when they do not listen to their child's need to have some degree of freedom to develop self-respect and personal responsibility, they can crush the spirit out of their child and leave her with the feeling that who she is as a person is not valued. Overcontrol undervalues the person being controlled. While appropriate limits help children develop, oppressive boundaries inhibit growth.

This was the case with Doris and Edward. If you asked Edward how he felt about his relationship with his mother, the last thing he would tell you was that he felt rejected by his mother or that his mother feared his rejection. Her overcontrol looked to Edward like the actions of a mother who loved him more than anything else in the world. Actually, even though he wasn't conscious of it, Edward feared his mother would reject him for not making up for his father's absence.

Another example of covert rejection occurs when parents give children uncontrolled freedom. Again, on the surface these parents may appear to trust their child's ability to decide for himself what behavior is best. Overly permissive parents may look like people who do not want to oppress their children with rules and restrictions. Paradoxically, this is not good for a child's development either.

121

Uncontrolled freedom can leave a child with the feeling that what he or she does or how he or she behaves doesn't really matter to anyone. This can also cause the child to feel like he doesn't matter. When parents don't set any limits, they can send the subtle message "I don't care" to their child, causing him to experience covert rejection.

Take Bobby, for instance, who was raised by his father and two older brothers because his mother left when he was young. Because his dad and brothers were busy at their jobs, Bobby was allowed to do pretty much whatever he wanted, whenever he wanted to do it. Not raised to have much of a concept of parenting, Bobby's dad didn't really know how to provide him with supervision. He expected Bobby to take care of himself and to ask if he needed anything. Although his dad meant this as a sign of love and trust, Bobby didn't experience it that way. If he stayed up late and missed school, no one noticed. If he didn't do his homework, it didn't seem to matter. If he experimented with drugs, nobody could tell. While Bobby's friends thought he had it made, Bobby just felt all alone. Eventually, Bobby started getting in trouble with the police. At least then he could get his father's attention, and that was the only time he felt like he mattered to the only parent he had left.

Of course there are many other ways children can experience covert rejection. The death of a parent, divorce, parents being too busy, or not paying attention are just a few of the reasons a child can feel rejected. The parent may not intend to make the child feel this way; in fact, the parent may genuinely love the child but be more concerned about his or her own agenda than the child's, or the parent may simply misunderstand the child. Whether intentional on the parent's part or not, children can suffer from covert rejection, which can be very difficult to understand because it is often not even acknowledged. Whether they are defending themselves against overt or covert rejection, as adults they can miss opportunities for intimacy by trying to earn love through "good" behavior. To heal from past wounds and to live fully in the present, we must learn how to face our fear of rejection and deal effectively with guilt.

HOW TO DEAL WITH THOSE WHO MISMANAGE GUILT

If managed effectively, guilt is an emotion that leads to the development of safer, more intimate relationships. Guilt, motivated by love, gives us the courage to be honest and the hope of forgiveness and reconciliation. We can learn to manage guilt with a sense of power and mastery.

How we use, or misuse, personal power will determine whether or not we manage, or mismanage, the emotion of guilt. When we insist on maintaining a balance of power in our relationships, we are less likely to be manipulated by the disapproval of others. We will be less likely to control others with our disapproval, as well.

Doris misused her power by dominating Edward, who in turn made unilateral decisions that were hurtful to Ann and his children. One day Ann decided to put an end to this and told Edward she wanted a divorce. Edward was stunned. After all, he saw himself as such a good and giving man. But at the threat of losing his family, Edward finally agreed to go to marital counseling.

During the next few months, Edward faced the fact that he was refusing to exercise his rightful power appropriately in his relationship with his mother. He also saw how he hurt Ann and his children by taking their power away. We'd like to say that once Edward had these insights, everything was great for this family, but that would be minimizing how difficult it can be to restructure longstanding and abusive relationships. Edward started by deciding to take the promotion offered to him and moving upstate. His mother felt terrible, cried, and indirectly blamed. Edward could not have withstood this barrage without the constant support of his therapist and wife. He even started attending a men's support group once he moved north, and these voices of sanity helped him retain his personal power.

The most difficult challenge for Edward was dealing with the guilt his mother heaped on him for becoming a man and "leaving" her. When parents do not want children to grow up, the children can feel like they betray their parents when they become the adults they were meant to be. Edward realized he could not stop his mother from blaming him. However, he learned how to tolerate his mother's attempts to heap guilt on him and did not buy into it.

He continued to care for Doris from a distance, coming to see her occasionally when he could. Because old habits die only when they are replaced by new ones, Edward was susceptible to Doris's manipulations for an extended period of time. At first, Doris moped, developed a variety of physical ailments, and called Edward at times she knew were inconvenient. But as Edward held steady, Doris began to look for attention elsewhere. Even though his mother continued to complain, she eventually started making new friends and joined a travel club. Now, from time to time, Edward gets a postcard from his mother from her travels. He pins them to the wall of his office as reminders that taking back his power really is a positive thing, even if it is painful at times.

Managed guilt respects the individuality of people, allowing them to be who they are and to live with the confidence that they are not going to be continually rejected because of it. Individuality may cause some differences between people, but these differences don't always lead to

124

disagreements. Differences may cause others to be hurt, but managing guilt means being confident that relationships are strong enough to survive these problems.

Insist On True Integrity

One of the marks of a mature person is having realistic expectations for one's self and for others. It is unrealistic to expect that we will go through life without making mistakes or hurting other people. We all get hurt somewhere along the way and we eventually hurt other people, whether we intend to or not. Coming to accept this truth is the first step in properly managing guilt when—not if—we fail to live up to our own standards or someone else's.

Knowing that you will fail and hurt others, even those you love the most, releases you from the false hope of being perfect. Rather than withholding love from yourself through self-rejection or living under the threat of punishment from others, it is critical to accept that difficulties will happen, misunderstandings will occur, disappointments are inevitable, and people will hurt each other. False integrity feeds off the illusion that it is possible to avoid doing anything wrong, while true integrity leads us to make amends once a wrong has been committed. Managed guilt plays an integral role in true integrity as it provides the motivation to restore relationships once they have been ruptured.

Does this mean you should simply abandon yourself to living any way you please, not worrying about how much damage your behavior causes? Are we implying that you should accept the hurt others perpetrate on you without making a fuss? Not at all. We are emphasizing that all of us fall short of how we would like to be. We cannot offer anyone a completely safe relationship, nor will we ever be able to find one. Being close to another person comes with risk of hurt. No one can live up to his or her own standards, let alone all the expectations others may have. Accepting this, it is important to have a plan for when we hurt others or they hurt us.

We need to make a commitment to the truth, seeing reality clearly, and telling the truth about what we see. Courage is a requirement for genuine integrity because the truth often leads us to painful places. Growth is both exhilarating and painful. Intimacy draws us close to comfort as well as the possibility of pain. Being a person of integrity does not lead to a painless life. On the contrary, legitimate pain and suffering are inherent in a life of integrity.

Learn from the Past, Stay in the Present
If we are going to talk about guilt, then we also need to talk about forgiveness, one of the most powerful tools in human relationships. There are two levels of forgiveness. The first level is the commitment to act in a way that does not return hurt for hurt. While you may feel angry, resentful, or even fantasize about revenge, you can choose to behave in a way that separates rather than embroils you further in the Victim Trap. Forgiving someone in this way can free you from endless turmoil, which otherwise can upset you for years. Eventually, release from feelings of pain and resentment comes.

The deeper level of forgiveness we will call reconciliation. This is when two or more people come to a mutual understanding of how they have been hurt and have hurt one another and express genuine remorse for it. This does not happen as often as we all need. Too often, we opt for a cheap counterfeit of forgiveness, pretending not to hurt as much as we do or minimizing how we have hurt others.

To forgive someone for what they have done to you without the assurance that they understand the depth of how you were hurt by them is not reconciliation. You are left with unresolved hurt and a mistrust of the other because you have no reason to believe they will not hurt you again in the same way. Coming to an understanding of the pain and responsibility means entering a shared reality that is the basis for a safe relationship in the future.

Doris never came to a deep understanding of how she had damaged Edward, so he was only able to forgive her on the first level. He set clear boundaries for himself, refused to take on her guilt messages, and accepted her for the emotionally damaged woman she was. He forgave her, but he didn't forget that as long as she remained in the Victim Trap she was dangerous to him.

Edward also gave a precious gift to his family. He gave them the opportunity to forgive him on the second, deeper level. He sat down with his wife and children, giving each an opportunity to express how he had hurt them. He listened and accepted their experiences as valid, even when their perceptions differed from his own. He didn't accept blame from his family nor excuse their behavior because they had been hurt. But he did take responsibility for harmful actions he had committed and worked to make amends with each person. This process created a new, shared reality in which he, his wife, and children were safe to experience both acceptance and differences. Rather than mismanaging his guilt and thereby alienating and hurting his family, he channeled his true guilt into reconciliation and restoration.

Managed guilt seeks reconciliation, motivating us to understand how we have hurt another because our remorse is real and we want to know how to avoid being hurtful in the future. This is not just about trying to be good or doing it right next time; it is about understanding feelings that have not yet been understood. This kind of guilt is based on love and wants to repair what has been injured, not just make up for what has happened in the past.

For example, Erick grew up resenting his father for sitting in front of the television drinking all evening, and then being both verbally and physically abusive to any family member who got in his way. Erick couldn't wait until he was old enough to leave home and get as far away from his father as possible. Once on his own, he was invited to attend a support group for adult children of alcoholics, which gave him understanding into his father's situation. But before Erick and his father could talk, his father was killed in an automobile accident.

Erick was no longer able to approach his dad with the kind of forgiveness that goes to the deepest level in relationships. He was, however, able to get help for himself through his support group. Erick spent months talking in the group about the anger, hurt, grief, and guilt he felt about his father. Even though it was too late for his father to benefit from it, Erick eventually forgave him with the help of others he could trust with his feelings.

Managing guilt means trying to get to the deepest level of forgiveness. This is more difficult if the other person cannot or will not cooperate with you. Sometimes others refuse to talk to you or are not able to understand the meaning of this kind of communication. Sometimes they are out of your life or even dead. You can still achieve a significant degree of forgiveness by dealing with the person you carry around in your head, the person you still have conversations with in your mind. You can also find tremendous help by dealing with this in a support group or with a trusted confidant.

Forgiveness works both ways; sometimes you need to forgive others and sometimes you need to allow others to forgive you. When you have legitimate guilt over past behavior, you need to come to a full understanding of how you hurt the other person and then realize the meaning of being sorry. Healing remorse does not only mean promising not to do it again; it means understanding the depth of pain you have caused. Whenever possible, have a conversation with the person you have wronged on a level of emotional understanding that acknowledges the depth of what you have done. This can give you the sense that you can now be forgiven at the deepest level. Whether the pain caused was intentional or not, you can make amends from the bottom of your heart. In the same way, truly reconciling with people who have hurt you requires that they understand your pain and express genuine remorse. Reconciliation includes trust that the past will not be repeated. Accepting anything short of earned trust is to foolishly set yourself up for revictimization.

We want to emphasize that reconciliation does not necessarily mean you invite someone back into your life or enter back into his or hers. Reconciliation is a mutual and compassionate understanding of pain. Even after you have forgiven someone to this depth, you may still decide that he or she is not welcome in your life. You do not need to refuse to forgive someone to keep him out of your life. You may decide to forgive someone and still set very clear boundaries. Some people are simply not good for you, even if you have forgiven them.

Perhaps one of the most difficult aspects of staying in the present requires releasing the fantasy of "potential." If you are waiting for someone who mismanages guilt to change, and you are doing this because of the tremendous "potential" you see in him or her, at some point (and we suggest that today be that day) you must decide how long is long enough. You may need to stop making excuses for why he or she is not changing. If you are living in the present, time is up for potential. Otherwise, you will live in frustration for tomorrow and continue to sacrifice today.

Take Responsibility and Hold Others Accountable

Since those in the Victim Trap can use guilt as a way to manipulate us, it's important to learn how to manage our own guilt effectively. Healthy guilt reminds you to finish

129

your unfinished business with those you love. Mismanaged guilt draws you into an endless Victim cycle. Remember, assigning blame never helps, especially when the target of blame is yourself. Since blame seeks punishment, blaming yourself keeps you stuck, and faultfinding becomes your central activity. Going over and over in your mind how you could have, should have, would have does not move anyone toward healing the hurts; it only throws you into an endless cycle of mismanaging your guilt. Blaming yourself gives you the illusion of being a person of integrity and the false sense of taking responsibility for your wrongdoing. Managing your guilt, on the other hand, takes the focus off blame and puts it on creating solutions.

As you sort through the guilt trips and realize you have genuinely wronged another person, it is important to acknowledge your hurtful behavior and explore how you can make amends for the damage you have caused. It was hard for Edward to face the amount of neglect and abuse he had perpetrated on his family. He set about making amends with each person, paying attention to individual needs and concerns. Not only did he apologize to his son for ignoring his need for fatherly support, he also made sure he attended all of his son's piano recitals from then on. After acknowledging how disappointed his daughter was to miss camp, he made sure he had enough money saved for the following summer. Ann was delighted to see the changes in her husband and thanked him with tears of joy when he whisked her away for a weekend alone. Because he had spent so much time with his mother on the weekends, Ann and Edward hadn't had time alone for nearly seven years.

Making amends means doing what you can to heal the damage you've caused and changing your behavior in the future. Merely asking forgiveness without making any changes is insufficient. The most challenging thing for

Edward was recognizing he had indeed failed his mother, although not in the ways for which she blamed him. He had robbed her of his honest feelings and the intimacy she had wanted but did not know how to receive. To the best of his ability, he acknowledged to her how he felt he had wronged her, even though she only partially listened. To take in her son's apology would have empowered Doris, yet she chose to hold onto her role in the Victim Trap rather than embrace an intimate relationship with her son.

While managing your guilt means taking responsibility, it does not lead you to grovel for forgiveness. This is another form of giving up your power and succumbing to the mismanagement of guilt. You need to be genuinely concerned about how you have hurt another, focusing on understanding the other's pain more than on making your own pain go away. But you are not responsible for doing penance for your wrongs. Taking responsibility is not as much about making things right as it is about making them better. This kind of guilt acknowledges when things cannot be fixed, but it never stops caring about it.

Paradoxically, once you accept the fact that relationships can be hurtful and require a balance of power, you make it less likely you will hurt others or be hurt by others. No longer motivated by fear of rejection, you are more able to tell the truth about yourself, your experiences, and your feelings. You become less vulnerable to others' misuse of power because you can stand in your own power and pull away to a safe distance if need be.

Sometimes you can protect yourself from revictimization by establishing new boundaries based on past experience. Using your power to face the truth, you no longer allow people into your life in the same way. As Edward faced the pain he had suffered from his mother's manipulations, he made a number of changes in the way he related to her.

131

For example, he limited the time he spent on the phone talking to her. Rather than answer the phone every time she called, he used the answering machine to screen the calls. He was quick to respond if she was sick or in real need, but on a regular basis he returned her calls when he had about twenty minutes to spare. Rather than continue as her round-the-clock handyman, he contracted with a management service to take care of her house. He also arranged with the local visiting nurse association for someone to come in to see her regularly and make sure she was eating well. A much deeper connection became possible when Edward started to set boundaries with his mother and not let their combined guilt dictate his actions. He actually started to enjoy his relationship with his mother when he limited the number of her requests he would try to meet. Once he held her accountable in this way, Edward could take responsibility for his part of the relationship. He was responsible for being honest with her and caring for her. He could not take care of her, but he could care for her. Although it was more difficult for Doris than for Edward, making this distinction led to a somewhat more intimate relationship between them.

When you have been harmed, redefining the boundaries of a relationship is necessary to avoid revictimization. While you cannot make other people understand how they have hurt you, or even care about it, you can exert your personal power and refuse to respond to their efforts to use guilt to control your behavior. Whenever someone else makes your decisions, you are being violated and will undoubtedly suffer the consequences.

Guilt after the fact is the beginning of integrity, not the proof of it. Being involved in a relationship where you constantly feel guilty is a signal for you. Guilt should alert you to the fact that you need to take responsibility for something—and it may not be what the other person wants you to feel responsible for. You must do the work of uncovering what your true responsibility is in the relationship.

PERSONAL REFLECTION

The best way to protect yourself from falling into the Victim Trap is to learn how to manage your own guilt well. If you make some of the same mistakes in thinking that characterize the Victim Trap, you will be a perfect partner in a guilt-infused relationship.

Think about a relationship in which you feel guilty, and reflect on whether or not you are mismanaging these feelings as you ask yourself the following questions.

What does this remind me of? Our tendency to mismanage guilt is usually the result of mismanaging emotions throughout our lives. How have you mismanaged guilt over your lifetime? What was it like for you as a child? How did your parents deal with guilt in their lives? How is the way you're managing guilt in your relationships today similar to or different from the way you managed guilt in childhood? Try to become aware of patterns of mismanaged guilt and how they may have gotten started for you.

What feelings am I experiencing now? Be honest. Mismanaged guilt tries to avoid feelings while managed guilt wants to bring them out into the open. It takes courage to face all of how you feel, but the rewards are worth it. Managing your guilt feelings means you want to know all of how you feel and all of how others feel, as much as possible. If you are doing things to try to avoid how you feel, then you are moving in the wrong direction. Ask yourself, "What was I feeling when I did that for her?" and "How do I feel now that I've done it?" Examining your real emotions is the first step in managing them and moving out of relationships with those who are mismanaging their own.

What feelings are underneath what I am experiencing now? This is always harder to answer. You may not be able to do this by yourself, so you may want to ask a close friend what he or she thinks might be going on for you. This is risky, so you will want to pick a trusted friend, and you may still need to brace yourself for the response. Ask if he or she sees anything about the way you deal with guilt in your life that he or she doesn't think you see. If you mismanage your guilt often, your friend might not want to be honest with you not wanting you to feel guilty about feeling guilty. But if you are really interested in growing in this area you may convince someone to help you out in this way.

Most importantly, ask yourself if your fear of rejection underlies the guilt you feel. Does your guilt come from your fear that you will lose what you have if you don't sacrifice for others? Which do you feel most, fear or love?

How can I best express my feelings to maximize healing and growth? Improving your ability to love and be loved is the best way to deal with your fears of rejection. This is more difficult in some relationships than others. There are certain people you find more lovable than others, and these are excellent people to have more of in your life. Learn from those who live by the adage, "Friendly people have friends." If you are aware by now that you are mismanaging guilt in your life, make it a point to focus on both the giving and receiving of love.

What about the other feelings you need to express? Managing your guilt means you are willing to deal with confrontation and anger. What is the best way for you to talk honestly with someone you fear is displeased with you? What are you feeling that you have not admitted? How have you misled the other into believing everything is "fine" when it doesn't really feel that way at all? Managing your guilt

134

means dealing openly with underlying feelings, not keeping them hidden because they are too painful to talk about.

How can I hold those who hurt me accountable for their actions? You may think you are the person who needs to be held accountable, but what you may need to hold yourself accountable for is to stop blaming yourself. How can you take the focus off what you did or didn't do that was wrong and put it on the giving and receiving of love in your life? Perhaps you need to hold yourself accountable to receiving more love than you are allowing in now. What can you do to improve your ability to receive love?

Are you mismanaging your guilt in any relationships now? How can you hold others accountable to being more honest with you about their feelings? Imagine how different Edward's relationship with his mother might have been if he had been able to tell her about his true feelings in their relationship. Making this shift from blaming himself to holding her accountable to talking about his innermost feelings might have entirely changed the way they related to each other. Do you have any relationships in which you avoid talking about how you feel in the relationship because you feel too guilty most of the time? Rather than blame the other person or yourself for making you feel this way, how can you hold him or her accountable to more honesty?

Do you have the feeling that you need the other person to "let you go" before you can stop feeling guilty? Mismanaged guilt is based on the belief that there is an imbalance of power in the relationship and you are powerless to get what you need from the other person. How can you hold the other person accountable to a mutual relationship between two adults, rather than continuing on in a parent/child dynamic? The deepest level of forgiveness is an exchange between two people of equal power who come to a mutual understanding of how they've hurt each other.

What is my responsibility in creating this situation? This is not a question about how you have been at fault, but how you can take responsible action to heal the hurt and change the imbalance of power in the relationship. It is more a question of what you are going to do than what you have done. With this forward-looking attitude, what can you take responsibility for that might bring about a positive change in the hurt feelings of others and yourself? What needs to be forgiven? Is reconciliation possible? Assigning blame to the person at fault is not important here; the real question is whether or not you are the one perpetuating the problem.

What can I learn from this situation? Edward needed to understand how he hurt Ann by mismanaging his guilt with his mother. While Doris felt powerless to be different, she exerted a powerful effect on everyone around her. Guilt is not simply a personal matter. It affects the people around us. Understanding how we affect those we love is imperative if we intend to manage our guilt. Doris was so caught up in the mismanagement of her guilt that she could only see the pain in her own little world, which blinded her and Edward to the pain they were causing Ann and the children.

How am I powerful in the situation? This is the crucial question for any person who wants to avoid falling into the Victim Trap. How is the way you're managing your guilt blinding you to your impact on others? What are the direct and indirect ways you might be influencing others? Examine how well you communicate your feelings to others, especially those who are guilt-ridden in your life. How can you make a difference by using your power more constructively? How is your guilt keeping you from giving to and receiving love from those around you? What resources do you have to change the way you operate?

How can I redefine the relationship? An important question to ask yourself is, "Can this person do business with me?" What this means is, can the person who mismanages guilt talk honestly about feelings and take responsibility for his or her part in the relationship? Will he or she blame you? The answer to this question is crucial because mutual relationships between adults require both parties to set healthy boundaries. The imbalance of power these individuals experience in their relationships is partly the result of entering into relationships with other people who seek an imbalance of interpersonal power as well, only they want the power to be mostly on their side. You may be trying to get someone to accept you who just can't. It may be a divorced spouse, a relative, or a former friend. If you avoid facing your feelings of rejection, you may keep feeling guilty. There may be relationships you simply have to let go.

If you have been mismanaging your guilt because you have been trying to get someone to fill in for a parent with whom you haven't resolved your issues, how can you redefine the current relationship so that neither one of you is in the parental role the majority of the time? How can you change the rules of communication between you and the other person? What needs to change so you can feel love more often than fear?

Mismanaged guilt feeds on itself. Because it is based on the fear of rejection, mismanaged guilt causes us to cover up feelings of powerlessness with agonizing protestations of good intent. Since the real problem is never resolved, we are trapped in an endless cycle of guilt and failed expectations. Managed guilt is based upon love, caring more about making things right than focusing on what went wrong. If you find yourself in the guilt-ridden Victim Trap, take responsibility for getting the help you need to manage your guilt effectively.

THE TRAP OF MISMANAGED ANGER

SAM WAS TIRED OF sitting in the living room late at night, feeling hurt, confused, and all alone. His wife, Marla, would be stomping around their bedroom, slamming drawers as she got ready for bed. They fought almost every night. This was getting really frustrating.

They'd been having these scenes more often ever since Marla told him she'd been molested as a child by some guy who lived in her neighborhood. Sam had listened, trying to be supportive and understanding, having no idea that married life as he had known it would be turned completely upside down.

After they began fighting, Sam met with Marla's therapist. Sam told them both that he thought he could handle this and be supportive of Marla. He did not view himself as some kind of jerk that forces himself on a woman, but he was starting to get angry himself over the constant rejection he was feeling from Marla. She seemed angry at him all the time now, and he wasn't the guy who'd molested her. Because of all that was happening to them now, Sam was sure of at least one thing: child molesters should be severely punished.

RECOGNIZING MISMANAGED ANGER

To effectively deal with people who feel powerless, it is important to understand how they feel, what they are trying to accomplish, and how they mismanage their emotional life. This is especially critical if they mismanage the emotion of anger.

Anger is a powerful emotion that can bring about great change or great destruction. Unfortunately, because Marla did not completely understand her anger, it became both a constructive and destructive force in her life. Marla was angry most of the time. Although she didn't like feeling this way, she was furious about what had happened to her, and it captivated her thinking at some point almost every day. While anger was a natural response to her childhood abuse, and could play a constructive part in her healing process, Marla's mismanaged anger had become destructive in her relationship with Sam.

Anger can be used constructively in our lives to help us resolve our unfinished business with people and move on. However, when anger is mismanaged, a number of negative consequences result that can be destructive to ourselves and to others. If you are in a relationship with a person who mismanages his or her anger, or if you mismanage your own anger, you need to recognize some possible consequences.

MISMANAGED ANGER BECOMES A WAY OF LIFE

The power of properly managed anger gives us the capacity to make necessary changes in our lives. However, mismanaged anger robs us of true power to live our lives in loving, effective ways. Marla had a definite sense of strength when she was angry at Sam, but this feeling of anger blinded her to the fact that she was powerless to behave in any other

140

manner toward him. She had no choice. Her fury dictated her actions. When anger is mismanaged, root problems are never identified. Instead, we can go off on a wild-goose chase, blaming others with fury but never resolving the pain. Marla curtailed understanding of her situation by simplistically deciding that all men were untrustworthy. Mistakenly, she thought the betrayal she experienced in her childhood proved that men could not be trusted. She thought she needed to understand why men behaved the way they did. But it wasn't men that Marla needed a better understanding of, it was Marla.

When we mismanage our anger we are unable to understand ourselves. We lose our definition of self in our hatred of others. Blaming others becomes our defining characteristic as traits like compassion, reasonableness, and sensitivity are eclipsed by our fury. What has been done to us, and how angry we are about it, becomes a huge part of who we are.

In the course of trying to heal from sexual abuse, Marla began to identify herself as a victim, rather than a survivor. While she had every right to be mad about the way she'd been victimized, as long as she saw herself as powerless she could not move on to any other understanding of herself and her pain. Her fears about herself, men, and her ability to deal with this kind of pain remained unresolved for Marla. If there was anything to learn about herself and how to relate to Sam today, Marla could not see it. The only thing she thought she'd learned was that she couldn't trust men.

Consider the following examples of how others became lost in their mismanaged anger:

~

Ken was never the same outgoing, carefree teenager he had been before the holdup. The mere thought of that man in

141

a ski mask holding a gun to his head and demanding his wallet triggered such rage in Ken that his hands shook. It was as if the mugger had stolen Ken's self-confidence when he took his billfold. Ken rarely saw his friends after the incident, preferring to spend nearly every afternoon at the shooting range practicing with his new handgun. He couldn't see that his anger at the man who robbed him was turning him into a man of violence.

~

Amanda stared at her mother's coffin, filled with anger that pushed out any sadness. As a little girl, Amanda had hated her mother for being "sick in the head." When she was little, her mother would swing between being loving and full of fun to being out of control with rage. Seemingly unprovoked, her mother would scream at her, break things, and make so much racket that the neighbors would come over. At the age of nine, Amanda moved in with her aunt because her mother had been taken to a mental hospital. She told her friends her mother had died rather than admit the truth. Now her mother really had died, but all Amanda could think of was how different, how much better her life would have been if it weren't for her crazy mother. She didn't miss her. She hated her.

~

As Marilyn angrily worked on the court documents, she heard Donald's voice in the back of her mind saying, "I can't take this anymore. Ever since the car accident, you spend all your time on this lawsuit. We never go out, we never have any fun, we never talk about anything else. I'm through with all this." Marilyn was furious that Donald had abandoned her a day before the case went to trial. "After all I've been through with this accident," she thought to herself, "I can't believe he was so selfish! This breakup is just another

loss I've suffered because of that accident, and boy am I
going to make that driver pay."

~

Anger, if used appropriately, can restore a sense of legitimate
personal power. However, mismanaged anger backfires, trapping us in a sense of powerlessness. Fooled by the intensity
of the feeling, we can believe mismanaged anger makes us
strong when actually it diminishes and damages us.

For example, as a little girl, Marla's sense of safety and
power was severely damaged by the neighbor who used her
sexually for several years. Believing she had no way to protect herself from repeated violation, Marla survived by cutting herself off from her feelings. Consequently, she entered
adulthood and her marriage numb to most of her emotions.
If she felt anything, Marla felt powerless and trapped in her
relationships with men. Although Sam didn't know it, Marla
had "performed" sexually, faking enjoyment out of a sense
of obligation.

As Marla unpacked the layers of her pain, emotions she
hadn't felt in years came upon her like flash floods. Unfortunately, Marla was unskilled in managing these emotions.
Instead of taking responsibility for her own emotions, she
often blamed Sam for whatever she was feeling. She used
these intense feelings as weapons against Sam in a misguided attempt to protect herself from further harm. And
when Marla vented her rage inappropriately at Sam, he was
confused as to how to protect himself without further damaging his wife.

Even though Marla felt threatened by the emotional and
physical vulnerability that was expected of her in her marriage, she failed to learn effective self-protection skills and
too often simply traded in her compliance for defiance. "I'm
never going to let a man hurt me again," she vowed to her-

self. Even though her commitment to stop the abuse in her life was an important one, she had a very difficult time uncovering the sources of her anger that had to do with her past rather than with her relationship with Sam. Without understanding her past abuse and retrieving the personal power she'd lost, she was unable to discern an intrusive touch from a loving caress in her current relationship. As a result, Marla found herself verbally assaulting Sam any time he approached her sexually.

Her angry outbursts made Marla feel powerful, at least temporarily. But she soon felt powerless again because she actually abdicated, rather than asserted, her power. Instead of being empowered by her anger to move forward in her life, she fell into the trap of angrily reliving her past victimization. Caught up in her mismanaged rage, it was impossible for her to differentiate between Sam's passion and the intrusion of her molester. When she felt Sam touch her, she experienced again the violation of her childhood. Determined never to feel overpowered again, Marla responded with fury. Her rage made her feel big. The cost, however, was the emasculation of her husband.

A sense of safety based on mismanaged anger does not last, nor is it truly empowering. In fact, Marla weakened her personal power by limiting her ability to perceive her options accurately. While temporarily feeling more powerful, she was actually less powerful, because her fury distorted her perceptions and actions. When Marla assassinated Sam's character, her chin stuck out with self-righteous pride. Even though she was damaging their marriage, she felt strangely better about herself for having hurt Sam. She believed her anger was reversing the perceived power imbalance between them. Fearing that women can be overpowered by men at any moment, she hoped that a furious woman would be a less attractive target for abuse.

144

Like Marla, we sabotage our efforts for self-empowerment by attacking others rather than by strengthening ourselves. When we mismanage our anger, we become blamers, furious at those who appear more powerful. The reason our sense of safety is so short-lived is that our personal power is never strengthened by mismanaging our anger. Rather, we simply violate others by trying to overpower them. The only truly satisfying solution is for us to empower ourselves rather than diminish others.

If you ever need to protect yourself from the mismanaged anger of another person, be mindful that your personal power will most likely come under attack. Many of your self-protective actions may be seen as threatening gestures of further abuse. Holding onto your own sense of safety can be a challenge in the face of raging accusations from someone who is mismanaging their anger.

Some turn their anger on themselves because they are so frightened of the destructive potential of their rage. Some refuse to feel angry at all, keeping this emotion stored within their bodies in the form of painful muscle tension, recurring headaches, ulcers, heart attacks, or even cancer. Always looking for someone to blame, they may blame themselves, turning anger into other self-defeating feelings such as anxiety, depression, self-doubt, resentment, or helplessness.

Others have so much anger bottled up inside that the slightest offense sets them off in outbursts that far exceed the current violation. Those who mismanage anger often seem to overreact to the actions of others because the current experience unconsciously reminds them of past abuse. It is important to recognize that you will probably be criticized for things that seem innocuous or harmless to you. Remember, this person believes he or she is fighting for survival and a sense of power, while you may be oblivious to the impact of your behavior.

Abuse begets abuse, anger begets anger. The more we use mismanaged anger to protect ourselves, the more likely we are to attract people who mismanage anger into our lives and the more likely we are to hurt and be hurt by others.

Mismanaged Anger and the Loss of Self-Esteem

Prior to facing her childhood molestation, Marla had seen herself as a competent, successful wife, mother, and career woman. She prided herself on having a successful fourteen-year marriage to a good man like Sam. Her three daughters seemed happy and successful in school. After her youngest went to kindergarten, she developed a catering business that blossomed, keeping her busy and excited about her work.

But somewhere in the back of her mind and memory, something never seemed quite right. At unexpected times, like during one of her catering jobs when things were going well, she'd feel overwhelmed by a sense of dread and terrible danger. Or if she caught the scent of a particular aftershave, she'd start to gag and have trouble breathing. Perhaps the most troubling times were when she made love with Sam and felt herself turn stone cold and "disappear" into the mattress. Marla was afraid she was going crazy, so she did her best to hide her feelings from Sam. She didn't want him to know how much she hated having sex with him.

When we are mistreated, especially if the violation occurs in childhood, it is common to feel damaged, defective, or worthless. As Marla struggled with the memories of her childhood molestation, she secretly wondered if somehow she deserved to be used in this way. Somehow she felt to blame. Remembering her abuser's invasive touch, she wondered if she'd ever enjoy sexual intimacy again. Fighting for her sense of worth, Marla became consumed with anger.

Anger is a healthy reaction to having something or

someone we value mistreated. The intensity of our anger can reflect the degree to which we care. If some possession has minimal value to us, we don't care if it's damaged or tossed out with the trash. But we get very upset if something we cherish is mistreated. If used effectively, anger can help us restore what has been taken or damaged. However, when we misuse our anger we simply do more damage. Like Marla, we channel anger not toward increasing self-esteem but in the fruitless pursuit of blame.

Marla verbally attacked Sam to avoid further injury. While she felt entitled to protect herself from the harm men could perpetrate, she also felt badly about being so vicious toward the man she loved. Each time she mismanaged her anger, more of her self-esteem was chipped away. The more she saw herself as being cruel, the less she esteemed herself. When she viewed Sam as being abusive and herself as the powerless victim, her self-esteem dropped lower still. The less she valued herself, the more she fell into the Victim Trap; the further she fell into the Trap, the less she esteemed herself.

Marla's mismanagement of anger is common for any of us who see ourselves as powerless. First, our self-esteem is undermined by the abuse itself. Next, our sense of worth and competency is further damaged by blaming others, rather than holding others accountable for their actions. In an effort to protect herself, Marla further damaged herself. By blaming her molester, her husband, and men in general for her troubles, Marla further convinced herself that she was incompetent, less than valuable, worthless, and deserving of mistreatment.

Sam's self-esteem was also damaged by mismanaged anger, as he often responded to Marla's anger with a rage of his own. At first he felt furious with her abuser and wanted to retaliate viciously against this man. He envisioned himself as Marla's protector and avenger, expecting her to be grateful to him for his efforts.

To Sam's surprise and dismay, Marla did not smother him with grateful kisses, but instead barraged him with criticism and fury. He felt frustrated and misunderstood. The more he tried to help, the more she raged. Falling into the "blame game," Sam began blaming Marla's past for all the problems in their marriage. He even found himself blaming her for somehow participating in the original abuse as his own mismanaged anger sought explanation for his pain.

When someone aims anger in your direction, your self-esteem, sense of self-worth, and even your identity are in danger. Like Sam, you may be asked to pay the price for what someone else has done wrong. Holding onto your sense of self can be difficult in the face of angry criticism, especially if there is even a hint of truth in the accusation. While Sam never molested a child or forced Marla to have sex with him, he was a passionate man who enjoyed making love with his wife. At times he was consumed with desire and intensity. Marla's angry response caused him to doubt himself and wonder, "Am I insensitive? Am I too demanding? Am I a rapist?" When anger is mismanaged, everyone risks getting hurt.

Anger is a powerful force in relationships. But like a surgeon's scalpel, anger can both heal and hurt. Self-esteem can be enhanced by managing our anger to create needed change and protect ourselves from harm. But we can feel badly about ourselves when our anger only serves to damage our relationships and our sense of competency. Managed anger asks the question, "How can things be better?" while mismanaged anger asks, "Who's to blame?" As Marla learned, her relationship with Sam was initially helped when she stopped pretending to be sexually intimate with him and insisted on a relationship of mutual respect. But over time, her mismanaged anger robbed her of the self-esteem she needed to be a fully authentic, personally powerful woman.

148

Mismanaged Anger Traps Us in the Past

Anger managed in a healthy way can help people move beyond the hurt of the past and create safety in the present. During the recovery process from abuse, there is a period of time in which it is appropriate to focus attention on the past. Survivors of abuse need clarity about what happened to them, who hurt them, and what impact this abuse has had on their lives.

However, when anger is mismanaged, problems do not get clarified. Rather, those in the Victim Trap become sidetracked into the "blame game." Let's look back at our previous examples.

Ken, the teenager who had been robbed at gunpoint, did very little to help himself heal from this trauma. Instead, he spent his time blaming the robber for everything difficult in his life, even the loss of his former friends. Ken could not see that his friendships were damaged, not because he had been held up but because he had become an angry, violent young man. His friends became afraid of him, not knowing how to help.

Amanda had, from girlhood, defined herself as the daughter of a "crazy woman" and then hated the label she had given herself. Because she was so consumed with blaming her mother for the losses in her childhood, Amanda was unable to gain any helpful perspective on her mother's illness or how to make her own life blossom in positive ways.

The car accident left Marilyn with huge medical bills and physical problems that would probably plague her for the rest of her life. The consequences of that terrible moment were tremendous and painful. But Marilyn only made her situation worse by intensely focusing her attention on blaming the other driver and making him pay, rather than finding ways to make her life as positive as possible. Without meaning to, she drove away a man who loved her

149

in spite of her physical problems. She chose blame over understanding the deeper feelings around her loss.

Healing from this kind of hurt takes time. Some people can work through this after several months, while others may need years. There is no specific time frame that works for everyone, no "right" way to heal. It certainly depends on the type of abuse, the age the person was when hurt, who perpetrated the abuse, and how people responded when the truth was told. Whether someone is recovering from childhood molestation, rape as an adult, divorce, or any other type of trauma, many people feel somewhat resolved after about two years of recovery. Some people recover more quickly, while others take many years to stabilize. But if any of us mismanage our anger rather than use it to move us through to resolution, we can become trapped in the past for the rest of our lives. This can occur in several ways.

First, *mismanaged anger chains us to our offenders.* Rather than using anger to distance ourselves from those who hurt us, to hold them accountable, and to provide the safety we need, mismanaged anger ensnares us in a web of blame. Marla's therapist wasn't alarmed when at first Marla thought about her molester many times every day. She thought about him when she woke up, during the day, and as she fell asleep. He even showed up in her dreams. But after a few years, it was clear that Marla was not using her anger to free herself; instead her anger strengthened the bond between her and her molester.

Second, *mismanaged anger forces us to relive our terror repeatedly without any release or healing.* Marla attended a support group for several years, retelling her story every time a new woman joined the group. At first this type of truth-telling is important and even necessary for healing. But Marla never moved beyond that stage. Instead, she became stuck in the past, continually defining herself

150

as the little girl who was overpowered by a man. Her mismanaged anger kept her from going deeper into her emotional life where she could become a strong and powerful woman who had survived a terrible experience.

Third, *we can be trapped in the past by embracing powerlessness as an identity.* Marla did not see herself as a competent adult woman. She lived her life as if she were a little girl, unable to protect herself from violation. Each time Sam touched her, she experienced his sexual advance as molestation, not an expression of love from a man to a woman. She unwittingly defined herself as powerless, so the only role left for Sam to play was all-powerful offender.

When we relate to those who mismanage their anger, their problems often become our problems; their mismanaged emotions often tag our weak areas as well. Sam was strongly impacted by Marla's mismanaged rage and, without meaning to, they engaged in a dangerous, angry dance. Marla obsessed on her molester; Sam obsessed on Marla. Marla repeatedly told her story with no resolution; Sam tried to get her to stop talking about it. Marla became entrenched in her powerlessness; Sam unwittingly used his power to force her to "get over it." But, of course, because Sam was not actually powerful enough to make Marla change, he sank into a smoldering state of powerlessness, falling into the Victim Trap himself.

This is common to most of us who deal with people in the Victim Trap. Because they feel powerless (and innocent), they treat us as if we are extremely powerful (and to blame). If we are susceptible to taking on too much responsibility for others, we may try to rescue or inappropriately defend these individuals. The problem with this plan is that it won't work. The belief that someone in the Victim Trap is powerless is a belief, not a fact. Sometimes it is hard to acknowledge that everyone has personal power because we can feel

151

needed by those who want us to somehow rescue them from their pain. But while we can support someone in exercising their personal power, we cannot "make" them heal.

Mismanaged Anger Underestimates the Damage Caused
Because we can feel so wounded and so powerless behind our anger, when we fall into the Victim Trap, we feel entitled to act any way we want. Believing we have minimal impact on others, we set few limits on our indignation and can feel entitled to anger in its most potent form. Having forcefully held our anger out of conscious awareness, it becomes transformed over time. When it finally does come out, it is expressed with self-righteous indignation such as, "I've had to take this long enough! Now it's my turn to be mad." Someone who believes she is powerless, like Marla, feels entitled to be as mad as she wants and even entitled to revenge with few limits.

Revenge is mismanaged anger seeking to return hurt for hurt. The goal is not healing, it's payback. Seeking revenge is a way of artificially balancing the scales, as if human suffering were something that could be measured out equally. It does make the avenger feel better, but only because it restores a sense of control and power that the avenger did not know how to achieve any other way.

Mismanaging anger keeps us from accurately understanding ourselves, our past, and our present. Whatever qualities of self-restraint and fairness we have previously developed are overshadowed by our fury. What abuses we have suffered and how angry we are about the past becomes a huge part of who we are in the present. Feeling wronged, we can feel justified in anything and everything we do. After all, we were victimized and now we are setting things right. Unfortunately, we lose an accurate definition of ourselves in the hatred of others as we incorporate our acts of cruelty into our self-image.

This was the case with Marla. She never perceived herself as critical or hostile. In fact, she thought of herself as forgiving of others, often to a fault. But her mismanaged anger erased graciousness from her personality. If Sam was inconsiderate, she experienced him as abusive and she felt the need to protect herself with rage. The more she mismanaged her anger, the more wounds she added to their relationship and the more her self-image was altered.

No matter how articulate or convincing we may be, it's important to remember that when we are in the Victim Trap, we do not have an accurate understanding of the past, ourselves, or others. Raging, we can cause immense damage to ourselves and to those around us by overestimating the power of others and underestimating the impact of our own behavior. If you have been the target of someone who mismanages anger, you may know the extent of this fury. Unable to see how you are hurt by their accusations or assaults, these individuals are rarely able to gauge how far is too far. And if you've been sucked into the mismanaged rage, you will also underestimate how damaging your actions are on others.

WHY DO PEOPLE MISMANAGE THEIR ANGER?

Why would anyone want to be angry in such a destructive way? Few people actually do. Most people mismanage their anger because they are flailing out in pain. When they were hurt, they concluded they were weak. Mismanaged anger is one way to defend against weakness and is an example of what psychologists call "a defense mechanism." All people use different kinds of defenses, especially in times of crisis. Defenses are necessary to survive. However, defenses can become problematic if used, not only in a crisis, but as a way of life.

153

While anger can be a constructive force in life, protecting us from violation, mismanaged anger is a defense mechanism that can cause serious damage. As we attempt to make up for a wound we received through mismanaged anger, we only cover the wound rather than open it up for cleansing and healing. Getting angry about being hurt can be positive if it empowers us to take care of the hurt, but mismanaged anger directs our attention away from the hurt and places it on some other object or person. This is a dead-end process that produces nothing constructive. Merely defending against the perceived source of the pain is not enough. It is also important to know what lies beneath the anger that keeps the embers glowing.

What lies underneath the anger? An honest answer to that question may reveal empowering information. If Ken had asked himself why he was so angry, he may have discovered he felt ashamed that another man had overpowered him. Amanda may have been able to acknowledge that underneath her anger was a deep embarrassment about her mother's mental illness. Rather than fume and rage and alienate the man who loved her, Marilyn may have been able to tell Donald that she was afraid he would leave her now that she wasn't as physically attractive or as strong as she had been. Marilyn's anger was a mask for the shame she felt about her body.

Several emotions can lead to anger, such as hurt, fear, and frustration. But one emotion leads to the mismanagement of anger more than any other—shame. Shame is difficult to deal with because it continually seeks to hide itself. This emotion strikes at the very core of our self-esteem and can cause us to act in ways that even we find disgusting.

Shame is different from guilt. Guilt is that uncomfortable feeling you get when you have gone too far or have not done enough. It is about our actions. Shame, on the other

154

hand, is the feeling of inadequacy for not being enough. Guilt is about what we do; shame is about who we are.

One of the difficult things about shame is that we often don't feel better by talking about it. Usually, to have someone point out that we are feeling shame about something is shaming. It is like having a spotlight shined on us when we're trying to hide in the dark because we feel underdressed or even naked. It makes us painfully aware of something we try to avoid noticing and also hope no one else will. As soon as we become aware of our shame, we usually try to hide from the pain of exposure. Talking about our shame often makes us feel defensive.

Shame was the root of both Marla's and Sam's pain and mismanaged anger. Neither Marla nor Sam ever came to an understanding of this because they were both distracted by her anger. They both thought focusing on the other's behavior was the solution to the problem. Sam believed that pressing her to heal faster, implying she wasn't healing the "right" way, was the right thing to do. Marla believed exposing men for the sexually selfish beings they are, for which they should feel guilty, was the right thing to do. In both cases, their anger was directed at punishing those they thought were to blame. This placed all their focus on assigning guilt and completely distracted them from the problem of shame.

Underneath Marla's protests of victimization lay a deep feeling of not being enough for Sam. She couldn't escape the thought that she was abused because she was bad. Even though she knew it was not her fault that she was molested, she somehow still felt it was. This created a terrible confusion in Marla's mind that she needed to resolve.

Sam also felt inadequate to be the kind of man Marla needed during this troubled period. Marla's sexual withdrawal and outright rejection embarrassed him. His shame

155

fueled his angry attempts to take charge and regain control of his wife and his bed.

Both Marla and Sam needed to deal with shame. Clearly, Marla was molested against her will. But looking back on it, she sometimes wondered if she could have done something different to protect herself. She even had the horrible thought sometimes that she may have partly enjoyed it and that was why it continued. These thoughts made Marla feel that she was a terrible person, which resulted in her intense feelings of shame. When she blamed Sam for her distress, he felt ashamed of his own perceived limitations and failings.

Unconscious shame plagued Marla because she believed her past proved that she was "damaged" and "worthless." Because she didn't feel protected by her parents, she felt that she was unlovable and undeserving of protection. Deep inside she believed that no one could really love her, and nothing Sam could do now affected this belief. She lashed out to punish Sam, magnifying his sense of "worthlessness" by rejecting him sexually.

Ironically, Marla's insistence that she was being victimized by Sam reinforced Marla's secret sense of shame. Each time she convinced herself he was uncaring or to blame, she was left with the nagging question, "Why is this still happening to me?" She couldn't see that she was doing anything to deserve this treatment, so she felt continually powerless. Tragically, this left Marla with the feeling that if it wasn't because of anything she'd done, then it must be because of who she was. It was as if she was defective inside, and couldn't help but attract abuse from others. In this convoluted way of thinking, those who blame others only intensify their own shame.

Marla felt she could do nothing to change things for the better; only Sam had that kind of power. After all, men are strong and women are weak, she told herself. Falling into the Victim Trap, her sense of shame was reinforced because she related to Sam, not as an adult woman of worth, but as a frightened, rejected child. Marla's mismanaged anger gave her the illusion of feeling "big" when inside she actually felt painfully small. She passed on a shameful sense of "smallness" to Sam. This fueled their mismanaged anger as it escalated in intensity and in a craving for revenge.

But revenge never heals shame, it only covers it up. Believing we are powerless contributes to feelings of shame. Add to this a humiliating event, and the feelings of shame become too intense to allow into conscious thought. Revenge offers feelings of control, self-righteousness, and powerful fury that eclipse the more painful feelings of shame. Then we don't feel powerless anymore. Revenge is a good cover-up but not a solution. "Getting even" is not the same thing as "getting over" a difficult situation.

Tragically, hiding shame keeps it repressed and causes it to come out surreptitiously in dreams, slips of speech, or behavior that everyone else except those in the Victim Trap can see. Sure, it feels better acting out revenge, but only on the outside. We are actually terrified of more hurt. The injury to date is too much to bear, so a wall of anger keeps out anyone who might pose a further threat. The wall works. It seals out injury, but it also seals out healing love.

The wall has another consequence. The human mind is an irrepressible thing. While shame may be too painful to openly express, that does not mean it silences us. Shame seeks to hide itself, but pain seeks to be known. When in the Victim Trap, we both hide and seek attention at the same time. In Marla's case, she tried to hide her shame and to express her deep hurt through her anger at Sam. Sam, unable to face his own sexual vulnerabilities, blamed Marla and her abuse.

This caused much internal conflict for both Marla and Sam. Even though they were furious, both felt that open expressions of anger were a sign of weakness and displayed a lack of control. A good person should not get angry or lose control. Because they did get angry and lose control, they experienced additional feelings of shame. Those caught in the Victim Trap of mismanaged anger invest a good deal of energy ineffectively battling shame and powerlessness, resulting in more shame and deeper feelings of powerlessness.

HOW TO DEAL WITH PEOPLE
WHO MISMANAGE ANGER

Sam confessed to his support group, "I get so angry with Marla when she criticizes me, especially if I haven't done anything wrong! I don't know how to handle it anymore. She gets angry, and then I get angry, and then she starts in again. We've become two of the angriest people I know!"

Sam's response to Marla's anger is typical. Have you noticed that it's easy to become angered when someone is angry with you? Anger escalates, especially when one person's anger stirs up another's anger in return. When anger generates more anger, the question becomes, "How can I manage my own anger effectively so that I protect myself but do not victimize anyone else?"

When you own your anger and use it well, you avoid falling into the Victim Trap. When managed effectively, your anger will give you tremendous energy to confront and solve the problems you face. It can give you the strength you need to take necessary action. Sometimes that action involves dealing with those who mismanage their anger. You can cut a new course for yourself, one that is empowered, balanced, strong, and fair.

What action do you need to take? What is the best way

to handle someone who has fallen into the Victim Trap? Some feel that the only way to deal with an angry person is to eliminate that person from their lives. While a physical separation may be possible, we do not believe that a psychological separation is possible without resolution at a deeper level. Once others have hurt us, they become a part of us. While we can never completely sever the psychological tie between ourselves and hurtful people, we can redefine destructive relationships so we are free from their negative impact.

Marla unwittingly used her anger to keep herself stuck in her relationship with her abuser rather than free herself from him. Sam, consumed with hatred for this man and eventually for Marla, was also caught up in Marla's rage. Their mismanaged anger kept them both connected to this abusive past relationship. They thought and talked about her abuser for years, trying to convince Marla that her relationship with him was over now. They missed the real solution: Marla's need to reclaim her power to redefine that relationship so she could feel safe.

How can we redefine and thereby disempower dangerous relationships? The most important thing we need to do is set new boundaries. Redefining relationships with people that we no longer physically have in our lives means realizing that we have the power to set our own boundaries in current relationships. Once she started facing her childhood molestation, Marla needed to take some time to decide for herself how she wanted to set sexual boundaries in her life. This meant backing away from all sexual activity for a while. She needed Sam to help her redefine what sexual involvement meant in her life, and for a while she needed Sam to be patient with her as she sorted that out.

Unfortunately for Marla, she mismanaged her anger to cover her shame about herself and couldn't make a crucial distinction in her sexual experience. Molestation is not about sexuality; it is about violence. She had been violated, and her abuser had caused her to confuse this violation with her sexuality. Marla needed to redefine this act of molestation as an act of violence against her, so she could redefine her sexuality now as having to do with love. Redefining the relationship in this way could have helped her experience her sexual relationship with Sam as something distinct and separate from her childhood abuse. Healing for Marla meant viewing and experiencing sex as a good and powerful part of her life. To achieve this, she needed to use her anger to redefine her past hurtful relationship and make her life safe enough to embrace her loving marriage.

Sam also needed to redefine his relationship with Marla by setting new boundaries. For example, in the past he had derived a sense of well-being and masculine confidence from his sexual experiences with his wife. Even though he would eventually again be able to freely and safely express himself sexually with Marla, for a while he had to redefine this part of their marriage and limit the impact of Marla's actions on his identity. While his wife was engaged in the important and necessary task of reclaiming her sexuality, he needed to find other ways to affirm himself as a caring and passionate man.

As he set new boundaries, Sam began to manage his anger more effectively. He used his anger to find a support group for himself, to provide emotional support to Marla, and jointly to confront her parents for not protecting her when she was a child. As he channeled his anger into action, he became more free of the past. Little by little, he let go of his own anger at Marla's abuser. As he learned how to protect himself from Marla's criticism and take responsibility for himself sexually, he expressed his anger in helpful rather than hurtful ways.

As you deal effectively with someone who is mismanaging anger, expect the unexpected. Often his or her response cannot be blindly trusted as a guide for your behavior. This was true for Sam. Oddly enough, rather than be grateful as Sam expected, Marla became angrier with him. She misinterpreted his lack of rage at her molester as betrayal and criticized him continuously for "not being a good husband."

Again Sam was challenged to use his anger for self-empowerment, this time to resist Marla's accusations that he didn't care about her. Instead of taking her blame at face value, he used his support system to sort out what was his responsibility and what was hers. He used his anger to hold her accountable for her actions and the ways she mistreated him. He needed his anger to create appropriate boundaries to protect himself from Marla's mismanaged anger.

While it is important to embrace your personal power, it is equally important not to overestimate your power. People can get hurt because they falsely believe they are so powerful that they can handle anything others dish out. This is especially true for men victimized by women who mismanage their emotions. In our society, we see men as stronger than women and unwittingly buy into the idea that women are powerless and therefore harmless. If you have made that mistake, you undoubtedly have a few emotional, and perhaps some physical, scars to show for it. All adults have personal power, regardless of gender, and you will put yourself in jeopardy if you underestimate other people's power and overestimate your own.

Furthermore, people have been hurt by those who mismanage their anger because they feel sorry for the hurt these people have suffered and therefore excuse their hurtful behavior. Too often people confuse forgiveness with making excuses for them, thus allowing them to continue their hurtful behavior. Sometimes being healthy means recognizing that certain

161

people draw you into the Victim Trap, and these people should not be allowed the same access to your life as they have had in the past. Sam had to learn how to protect himself from Marla. Forgiving others is not the same thing as inviting them to stay or allowing dangerous people to continue to be abusive. No one is helped if you ignore reality. If others are hurting you, no matter how much they've been hurt in the past, it is important to you and to them to tell the truth and to act on that truth.

Manage Your Anger

If someone scratched the paint on your car, you would probably be angry. If your car was old and beat up, you might not feel as upset as you might if you'd just driven a new car off the lot. The intensity of your anger would reflect the severity of the damage to your car and the value you place on your car.

This principle holds for how you treat yourself as well as your belongings. If someone blames and mistreats you, even if out of misguided pain, it's appropriate for you to feel upset. Your anger reflects the severity of your pain and affirms your intrinsic worth as a human being.

When criticized or blamed, it is also natural to doubt yourself. While it is critical that you take responsibility for your actions, it is also important to protect yourself from destructive criticism. If you have an ongoing relationship with someone who mismanages anger, you will need ongoing support to maintain a positive sense of self-worth and to cope with the anger you feel regarding their hurtful actions toward you.

We recommend that you channel your energy into cultivating your self-esteem. Make time to do things you genuinely enjoy and that give you a positive sense of yourself. If you love playing basketball, dancing, painting, or walking along the beach, take the time to do these things. You deserve it.

We've also found it helpful to get as many "reality checks" as possible when under the attack of mismanaged anger. Keep in touch with your friends rather than isolate yourself in shame and self-doubt. It can be especially helpful to talk with people who have known you for a long time and can remind you of your history, your strengths, and your positive attributes. Also, a professional therapist or support group can be of great assistance. These include groups for spouses of sexual abuse or rape survivors, Adult Children of Alcoholics, Al-Anon, Codependents Anonymous (CODA), or divorce recovery programs.

When you ask for support, open yourself up to constructive criticism as well as affirmation. Your self-esteem will be strengthened as you deal effectively with reality. In the face of mismanaged anger, you will be better able to keep your bearings and hold onto a realistic view of yourself as you receive reliable feedback from others. With support, you'll be able to navigate the confusion and distortions more easily.

While we recommend that you remain open to feedback and support from others, we do not recommend that you give the same credence to someone caught in the Victim Trap with you. If this person moves out of the trap and embraces his or her personal power, the feedback will become more reliable. But as long as their perceptions are skewed, it is impossible for him or her to accurately tell you anything about yourself. What you can be certain of is that this person has been hurt, is currently in a lot of pain, is unaware of unconscious motivations, and doesn't usually have a clue about how much he or she harms you. Many of the things you will be accused of feeling or doing will reflect more on his or her reality than on yours.

163

For example, when hurting people enter into therapy for the first time and begin to take their pain seriously, often they seem almost worse for having gone for help. While going to therapy can be an important first step in the recovery process, the changes experienced can be confusing at first. If someone in your life tells you, "I have a right to my anger" and "My therapist says it is progress for me to express my anger at you," do not take this as meaning the problem is yours. Nor does it mean the therapist condones any of this person's hurtful actions. When hurting people start to deal with their feelings, they can be somewhat clumsy at expressing their anger. Anger needs to be expressed, but it requires skill to learn how to do it constructively.

Your self-esteem will be best supported if you recognize that no one, not even you, is perfect. No doubt you have done things you regret, said things you'd like to erase, and ignored things you wish you'd acted upon. So join the human race. Success is learning from your mistakes, not avoiding them.

Learn from the Past, Stay in the Present

When confronted with mismanaged anger, you can be transported into the past as well. Just as the person mismanaging anger needs to face the past honestly and courageously, you may also need to start your own healing journey. With the help of a therapist and support group, we recommend that you take the time to heal from your past wounds if these are brought to consciousness by angry people. Remember, if you find yourself drawn into the Victim Trap by angry criticism, that wound is about your past, not the person verbally attacking you.

To resist becoming embroiled in the past of someone who mismanages anger, it is important to stay in the present while acknowledging your own areas of woundedness. When you are victimized, you naturally feel many emotions: confusion, sadness, loss, helplessness, shame, guilt, fear, anger, neediness, and longing. All of these feelings are legitimate and important because they reflect genuineness. When you are mistreated, you are not given the respect, protection, and honor you deserve, and that evokes many emotions.

It is important to take the time to feel your emotions, all of them. Some people resist experiencing their feelings because they believe they will then have to behave in a particular manner. This is especially true of anger. Many people are afraid to feel angry because they believe they will somehow be forced to hurt others. Simply feeling an emotion does not demand any particular course of action. Feelings and behavior are two different things.

Feelings are complex, often layered, and can be used to defend against deeper feelings. Underneath anger may be shame, hurt, or a sense of betrayal. Underneath shame may be loss, confusion, or abandonment. The better able you are to experience all the feelings you have in the present, the more empowered you will be when it is time to take action. You will be clear about who you are and what you need. The more you feel your feelings, the stronger and safer you become.

A good question to ask yourself when you get angry, especially if you find yourself in the Victim Trap, is, "What else am I feeling now?" In most cases you will find an underlying emotion like hurt, fear, frustration, or shame. The energy your anger gives you can help you take care of the problem that is causing one of these emotions in your life. Merely staying angry rather than exploring your deeper feelings limits you to a superficial understanding of them and prevents you from finding real solutions. The more you know about how you feel and how these feelings relate to past hurts, the better able you are to solve your problems.

165

Instead of staying angry at Sam, Marla could have asked herself, "What else am I feeling now?" Along with her anger, she might have discovered that she experienced Sam's need for sexual intimacy as a demand. Feeling required to surrender herself to a man was at the heart of her feeling abused. To move into intimacy based on personal power, Marla needed to express her anger and her accompanying emotions as well.

Once you have identified the feelings underlying your anger, you are in a better position to know if the action you take will be hurtful or helpful. Anger based on shame tends to be hurtful, but anger based on love tends to be helpful. Anger and love are not mutually exclusive. The anger needed to redefine a relationship can make way for more love in your life by making relationships safer. The anger used to cover over shame distances people from each other and shuts love out. Anger must not be avoided, it must be managed to resolve whatever unfinished business is at hand.

Take Responsibility and Hold Others Accountable
Because anger is so powerful and potentially destructive, it is best expressed and then quickly released from our systems. If we do not use anger immediately to create and strengthen boundaries and then promptly release it, this intense energy stays with us. Anger does not evaporate like steam. To the contrary, anger, like all emotions, insists on being expressed somehow, someday.

It is especially important to evaluate your actions when you are angry, to make sure this energy is being used to take care of the real problem rather than merely seeking revenge. There is no one less free than a person seeking revenge, and no one less satisfied, as Ken, Amanda, and Marilyn discovered.

Ken invested his money in buying more guns and his time in practicing his aim. His fantasy was to meet up, someday, with the man who had robbed him and shoot him in the head. Ken clung to the delusion that once this was accomplished, his life would be back to normal. As long as Ken invested his energy in revenge rather than in accountability, however, he would never get his power back, no matter how many guns he owned or how many bull's-eyes he hit.

Amanda's hatred for her mother did nothing to help her live a more loving and enjoyable life. In fact, she sabotaged her chances for happiness by becoming a resentful, critical woman.

Having won her case, Marilyn left the courtroom expecting to feel jubilant. After all, she had made the driver pay handsomely for the accident. But as she walked to her car, she didn't feel the satisfaction she had fought for. Instead, she felt alone, ugly, and resentful.

While Marla needed to face herself more honestly and stop blaming Sam, and men in general, for her feelings of shame and anger, Sam also needed to take responsibility for what he had done to exacerbate the situation. Returning anger for anger, criticism for criticism, many of Sam's initial responses were hurtful and made the situation worse. None of us can make others happy or stop them from feeling their anger. What you can do is face your own feelings and use your anger effectively. You can be honest about yourself and make amends for the true damage you've caused.

Holding others responsible when they hurt you is a necessary step in setting healthy boundaries. Anger is the energy you can draw upon to make needed changes and to set and protect your boundaries. You allow yourself to be revictimized if you do not restructure the relationship between you and the person who continues to hurt you. You cannot control others or stop them from being abusive, but you can hold them accountable for their actions and set up new boundaries that protect you from attack.

Redefining a relationship means recognizing how someone is hurtful and setting appropriate boundaries based on this knowledge. That may mean limiting the time you spend with this person, the places you go together, and whether or not you are ever alone together. Redefining a relationship requires wisdom, which means benefiting from experience. When you redefine relationships you experience yourself as powerful because you are in control of the definition.

How do you set new boundaries? You may need assistance sorting out specifically what will create safety in your situation, but here are a few ideas we've seen prove effective:

- ▶ Call "time out" when discussions escalate to destructive anger, always agreeing on a time and place to continue the conversation later.
- ▶ Decide to discuss past abuse only in the presence of a therapist or moderator so that both parties feel protected from the angry blame of the other.
- ▶ Clarify the "rules" of communication: don't blame, do get to the underlying feelings, and stick to the point.
- ▶ Decide not to talk directly; limit contact to letters.
- ▶ Refuse to answer the phone at all hours; set specific times you can be reached.
- ▶ Put physical distance between you by moving, changing the locks, or getting a restraining order.

Channeling any emotion into action can be positive and healing. Anger especially can bring about change and is most necessary when the pain you suffer comes from people you are in contact with on a regular basis, such as family members, friends, or coworkers. You must take whatever steps are required to protect yourself and provide a safe place in which to heal from loss and hurt. By calling on all the energy you can draw from your legitimate anger, you can protect yourself from repeated abuse.

It is especially important to follow the steps for holding people accountable when you are dealing with someone who mismanages anger. They can help you heal past hurts and avoid victimization in your relationship today. If you are stuck in an angry exchange with someone, follow these steps:

1. Describe the event about which you feel hurt and anger. What specifically happened?
2. Describe the meaning this had for you. How did you feel?
3. What can be done to make amends? This is not balancing the scale or getting even. It is repairing the damage so the wound can begin to heal.

Sam used these steps by describing their pattern of arguing right before bedtime. Without blaming Marla for these arguments, he told Marla how these arguments impacted him. He told her that he felt rejected and shut off from the woman he loved. While he supported her in feeling whatever emotions she had, including anger, he asked that they work together on finding ways to mend their relationship so that they both felt honored and empowered in the marriage.

When managed with skill, anger gives energy to take care of a problem. Taking responsibility for your feelings in your relationships is imperative to accomplish this, as well as holding others accountable for theirs.

PERSONAL REFLECTION

Are you involved with someone caught in the Victim Trap, or do you have someone in your life who is temporarily angry over being victimized? If you are dealing with someone who is trapped, then his or her anger is chronic and repetitive. If you are dealing with someone in temporary crisis, then his or her anger will not last forever. It is impossible to say exactly how long some anger will last, but people were not made to be angry all the time. Here are some questions that should help you to evaluate your personal situation, and what your own responses may mean.

What does this remind me of? When you experience intense feelings, you are often triggering emotions from the past as well as from the present. When anger or overwhelming frustration sweep through you, it is important to ask yourself, "What does this remind me of?" Perhaps you will remember a time when you were a teenager and someone made fun of your body or the way you looked. A memory of someone touching you in uncomfortable ways may come to your mind. You may hear a cruel voice of someone in your past saying you're stupid, ugly, or weak. The smell of cologne or body odor may signal an abusive past experience.

When you ask yourself what your current feelings remind you of, your body and your unconscious mind will struggle to provide you with an answer. Before you pretend to know what something means to you in the present, it is critical that you first understand what it has meant in the past. Like the old saying, "Nobody forgets where they buried the hatchet," you may have past hurts you think are resolved, but current circumstances remind you of them. This does not mean you didn't do everything possible to finish your business, it simply means that something new has happened and you are now aware of unresolved feelings. If you are reminded of past events, there may be an emotional connection between now and then that can help you sort out your anger and manage it well in your relationships.

What feelings am I experiencing now? Answering this

question is especially important when dealing with those who mismanage anger. Anger is such a powerful emotion that it is likely to bring up strong feelings in you when you experience it in others. Are you angry? It is not uncommon to get angry when you are confronted with anger. Are you feeling guilty? Sometimes, if we are caught in the Victim Trap, we begin to feel we have done something wrong when mismanaged anger is directed at us. This was the case with Sam. His mixture of anger and guilt made it difficult to sort out exactly what he was feeling in response to Marla. Take some time away from the situation and try to sort out your feelings.

What feelings are underneath what I am experiencing now? Anger is usually a response to a deeper feeling. In most cases, you can find hurt, fear, shame, or frustration just below the surface when you are angry. When anger becomes habitual, then other emotions become prominent, too. What is underneath your own anger? What is your first emotional response to the angry people in your life? Now what is underneath that?

How can I best express my feelings to maximize healing and growth? People get angry because something important is going on. Marla was not angry because her sexuality was unimportant to her and she wanted Sam to forget about it. Quite the contrary, she was angry because she was in pain over a very important area of her life.

Maximizing healing and growth means recognizing what is important and trying to bring as much energy as possible into those areas of your life. Knowing how you feel and what lies underneath those feelings, what is the best way to bring healing into the important areas of your life? Is the anger in your relationship pointing you to an important area that needs healing? How can you express yourself without doing more damage to the relationship and instead provide an opportunity for positive change?

171

How can I hold those who hurt me accountable for their actions? Angry people often hurt people. Sometimes they become addicted to the false sense of power that comes with mismanaged anger and they are angry most of the time. If you are in relationships with people who mismanage anger and you cannot physically remove yourself from the relationships, then you have the responsibility to hold them accountable for their hurtful actions. As mentioned earlier, remember to follow these three steps:

1. Describe the hurtful event specifically. Don't make general statements about how hurt you are or blame anyone else for your feelings.
2. Describe the impact of this behavior on you. How did you feel about it? What meaning does it have for you?
3. What can be done to make amends and reconcile the relationship? Be open to creative alternatives to accomplish the goal of healing. This is not an opportunity for you to control others or hold them hostage with emotional blackmail.

Following these steps can help you confront people who mismanage anger without further shaming them. The goal is not to make them feel bad about themselves but to make your relationships better.

What is my responsibility in creating this situation? When someone tells you that you're being hurtful, and that someone is very angry, you can get very confused. Anger turns up the volume on conversations, and the points you need to hear can get masked by the intensity of the dialogue.

Listen through their anger and try to agree on the points you think are legitimate. Don't throw everything out because you are on the receiving end of anger. Accept what you

172

think is true and sort out the rest.

Now, what do you want to do? Your responsibility is to be truthful about your feelings and take constructive action in the relationship. You are responsible to set your own boundaries and remind others when they have crossed them.

What can I learn from this situation? This is a very important question when you're dealing with anyone who mismanages anger. Anger directs you to a problem, and sometimes it takes anger to get the problem into the open. What did you learn about your situation that you didn't know before? What was underneath the anger that couldn't come out until you were too angry to keep it in? What is your own anger telling you about your deeper feelings and what action you might need to take?

How am I powerful in the situation? Marla's belief that she was being revictimized by Sam blinded her to the power she did have. It also allowed her to become vicious in her attacks on Sam because she did not believe she was powerful enough to make a real impact. Realizing that she did have power to hurt may have led Marla to the realization that she also had the power to heal.

Realizing that you are not powerless does not mean you can prevent yourself from being hurt. Sam was not giving Marla power over him by admitting that he was hurt by her actions. When you care about someone, you make yourself vulnerable to being hurt by them. Sam felt hurt by Marla's anger about his sexual desires, but this was not something he could just agree to leave out of their marriage. He had to stand in his power by being honest with Marla about his feelings and desire for change in their relationship. Powerful people get hurt, too. But powerful people are able to do something constructive after they have been hurt.

Once you have identified the feelings underlying your anger, ask yourself, "What power do I have to solve my problem?" Identifying your resources for power will help you identify what action you now want to take.

How can I redefine the relationship? Is this someone you want to have regular contact with? Just because Marla was angry did not mean that Sam no longer wanted a relationship with her. If this person is important to you, then you need to redefine the relationship in ways that make it safe for both of you.

What can you do to restructure your time together so that no one gets hurt? Do you need to limit certain conversations to times when someone else can referee for you? Do you need the help of a therapist or support group? Do you need to set new ground rules for communication? When dealing with someone who mismanages anger it is sometimes useful to agree to three simple rules of communication:

1. No blaming. This means use "I" statements instead of "You" statements. For example, say how you feel, such as "I feel angry," rather than "You make me angry."
2. Stick to the point. Don't bring up related events when you are trying to solve a specific problem. Fix one thing at a time.
3. Feelings first, then facts. Don't use facts like a lawyer trying to win a case to support your feelings. Just admit how you honestly feel first; it will save a lot of time.

Mismanaged anger is like a drug. Some people might even be thought of as "rageaholics" because they use anger to avoid other painful emotions. But, like a narcotic, this kind of anger covers rather than resolves the problem. The hard work of getting beneath the anger, often uncovering shame, is our way out of the Victim Trap.

6

THE TRAP OF MISMANAGED GRIEF

IT BROKE KATRINA'S heart when she thought about the divorce. Her greatest source of joy had now become her greatest source of pain. Martin had once made her heart come alive, and now he was breaking it. She felt lonely and afraid, and it didn't seem like anything would ever change that.

This wasn't the first time Katrina had been abandoned by the most important man in her life. In fact, the sick feeling she felt now in the pit of her stomach was exactly how she felt as a child every time her father was late picking her up from school or forgot her altogether. She was all too familiar with trying to comfort herself with statements like, "It'll be all right. He'll come soon," or "Don't cry. You're a big girl, and you can handle this." Katrina's relationships weren't fair. Why couldn't she count on the men in her life?

Nothing seemed to help. Mara, her best friend, tried to reach out to her, but Katrina just kept putting her off. She didn't want to be with anyone if she couldn't be with Martin. Mara's marriage seemed like a good one, and it only served to remind Katrina that she had failed in hers. She hated feeling so sad all the time, but she didn't want to be around a bunch of smiling people with their "oh-so-happy" lives either. She didn't know if she would ever get over Martin. He was the only one who could help her now.

RECOGNIZING MISMANAGED GRIEF

How do you relate to someone you love who is grieving a serious loss? What do you do when you try to understand the pain and end up feeling shunned? When you try to help, do you feel blamed for not ending the suffering? Have you ever been rejected by the person you are trying to comfort? Is it hurtful to be around someone who is grieving? We believe that it can be, if the person grieving perceives himself or herself as powerless.

We all grieve when someone we're attached to moves away from us in some way. This movement "away" can be a short distance, as in the case of a friend who still offers friendship but is no longer willing to have the same level of closeness or intimacy as before. Or the movement can be as extreme as death, in which someone important has "moved" completely out of reach.

Losses come about through natural and positive life changes, such as leaving friends when we go off to college or getting that promotion we wanted but finding we must move out of state to stay with the company. Other losses are the result of abuse or other "unnatural" experiences, such as physical injury due to being mugged or the loss of innocence due to childhood sexual abuse. All of us must face losses and the feelings these losses bring with them.

When we grieve, we ask questions: "How could God let this happen?" "Why did she leave me when I needed her so?" "Can I trust anyone to stay with me?" These kinds of questions can be gut-wrenching because they reach into the core of our being. Those in the Victim Trap tend to find dark, self-defeating answers to the natural questions evoked by loss rather than healing and comfort. When grief is mismanaged, a number of negative consequences result, consequences you must recognize if you want to deal effectively with someone who is mismanaging grief.

Mismanaged Grief Can Become a Way of Life

All losses are hard to accept. Perhaps it is easiest to deal with losses that are consequences of your own choices, because you retain a sense of personal power. While you might miss your friends and family while taking a three-week vacation in Europe, the pain of that loss is tempered by the knowledge that you made the choice to travel and that you can, at any time, decide to return home.

However, if you are the one left behind while your friends or family travel for three weeks, the same loss of contact may feel more painful. Along with missing your loved ones, you also feel powerless to make things different and perhaps devalued since you were left behind.

The losses that can seem the most difficult to handle are those over which we experience little or no control. A heavy, oppressive sense of powerlessness can descend over us, convincing us there is nothing we can do to stop the pain. Katrina had spiraled down in her grief to a place where she was convinced she was powerless, unloved, unlucky, and to be pitied. Rather than empower herself with a sense of competence and the will to build a new life for herself, she gave all her power to Martin. She decided that only he could make her happy and that she would never be happy again unless he came back to her. Consequently, grief became a way of life.

Furthermore, she took away the power of her friends. Mara, a longtime friend, was available to help her through her pain. But Katrina wouldn't let Mara comfort her in any

177

way. As a consequence, Mara suffered the loss of Katrina's friendship and the opportunity to care for her friend.

When we mismanage our grief, we create more losses than are necessary for ourselves and for others. Everyone suffers. Katrina made sure Mara suffered by withholding her friendship, illegitimately blaming Mara for her pain, and being unwilling to let Mara have her own feelings and losses. Katrina victimized Mara by the way she mismanaged her grief.

The sense of powerlessness can be compounded if a significant loss occurred in childhood. Children draw conclusions about themselves and about life that may last for the rest of their lives. For example, Jerry was only seven years old when his father died and his uncle told him by the graveside that he was the man of the house now. Jerry not only buried his father that rainy October afternoon; he also buried his own childhood. He was a little boy with no idea about what it meant to be a man. His uncle's words overwhelmed him, leaving him feeling confused and powerless. But he believed his uncle and did the best he could to assume responsibility for his mother and younger brothers.

With his childhood, Jerry lost the belief that anyone would be available to give him emotional support during stressful times. Jerry grew into a man ready to help others but unable to receive love from others. In fact, he rarely allowed himself to feel any emotions at all because a deep sadness and vulnerability would descend over him. No matter how many people depended on Jerry's help, inside he was a lonely man who tried to hide his sense of powerlessness and sadness by pretending to have the answers for everyone else.

Losses that occur in adulthood can also shake our sense of personal power and cause us to mismanage grief as a way of life. Melinda, a successful attorney, used to project a strong, self-reliant face to the world until the night Grady, an associate in her law firm, forced her to have sex with him at the end of a date. She stumbled out of his apartment dazed, unclear about what had just taken place. Somehow she made her way home. Her next memory is of sobbing in the shower, trying to wash his smell and the feel of his hands off her body.

Others in her law practice started commenting on how Melinda had lost her edge. She didn't seem to fight for her clients with the same daring for which she was known. When asked if anything was wrong, she tried to laugh it off. She couldn't admit to herself that she had been raped, let alone use her personal power to advocate for herself. Instead, she redefined herself as powerless and sank into a grief that left her immobilized.

A person need not be raped to feel powerless in the face of loss. Earthquakes wake us in the night, shaking homes from foundations and shattering a sense of personal power. Floodwaters break through carefully engineered dams, washing away businesses, schools, and the sense of security. More and more Americans are purchasing guns as they lose confidence in our police departments. Every day we are challenged with losses over which we have minimal control.

If we grieve courageously and effectively, a sense of equilibrium can be restored. However, mismanaging an emotional response to these losses can further disempower us rather than equip us to cope effectively with change. Rather than learn and grow stronger from difficult situations, we can make a lifestyle out of mismanaging grief.

Unrealistic Expectations
Since our perceptions are distorted when we fall into the Victim Trap, we rarely have realistic expectations of ourselves or of others. We expect both too much and too little.

First, we expect too much from ourselves. Stuck in low

179

self-esteem, Katrina believed that she was taking too long and should be able to "get over" Martin quickly and get her life back to "normal." So she blamed and shamed herself for the feelings she was having. She also misinterpreted Mara's frustration with her, concluding that Mara wanted her to stop being so sad. Katrina did not see that Mara simply wanted to be invited in to share the pain with her.

Second, we expect too little from ourselves. Like all who have fallen into the Victim Trap, Katrina saw herself as powerless and therefore abdicated any sense of responsibility for coping well with her grief. When we see ourselves as truly victimized, overpowered, and pitiable, we cannot imagine that anyone would expect us to take strong and healthy action on our own behalf. When Mara made various suggestions such as encouraging Katrina to talk about her feelings, go to a therapist, explore antidepressant medication, or simply go out to lunch to get out of the house, Katrina felt Mara was asking far too much of her.

Third, we expect too much of others. With an odd twist of self-importance, we can often see ourselves as the most pitiful, the most needy, and the most important. We expect others to view our needs as primary, to respond only to our pain. Katrina illustrated unrealistic expectations in several ways. Since she gave Martin complete power over her happiness, she expected him to come back to her and make things right. Furthermore, she expected Mara and all her other friends and family members to suspend their needs because she felt hers were so much more important. We can hurt others by ignoring or minimizing their feelings or experiences. Katrina not only dismissed Mara's sense of loss but also blamed her for expressing her feelings of sadness.

Finally, we expect too little from others when we fall into the Victim Trap. Lost in our sadness, convinced that no one but the "lost loved one" can restore happiness, we are

180

unable to receive the comfort and solace that is genuinely available. Mara couldn't bring Martin back, but she could help Katrina in many ways. She could sit with her as she cried, help her make decisions about the divorce, rent a movie and pop popcorn, and give her support as she started dating again. Katrina gave all her power to Martin, leaving herself and her friends helpless to ease her pain.

Mismanaged Grief Traps Us in the Past

Grief is a natural and necessary emotion when grappling with abusive or traumatic experiences. We feel sad, our hearts ache, our energy level drops, the slightest thing can bring tears to our eyes. These are natural expressions of grief. Healthy grieving takes time and is rarely resolved quickly. While there is no perfect time frame for grief, the "two years to recovery" idea can serve as a rule of thumb for major life losses. Smaller losses will take less time and larger losses may take many years to resolve.

While grief is intended as a transitional part of the healing process, those who fall into the Victim Trap get stuck in their sadness. Long after the loss occurs, those who mismanage grief may still sleep long periods of time with little interest in life, or they find sleep fitful and anxious. Emotions may be dampened by an overwhelming sense of hopelessness.

Some get stuck in their sadness because they simply refuse to let go. Rather than accept their losses, they use their feelings to hold on to the person or situation that is no longer available to them. Unwilling to accept the fact that they are divorced, that a parent has died, that they've lost their job, that their house has burned down, those caught in the Victim Trap dig in their emotional heels. By holding onto the sadness, these individuals try to hold onto what they've lost.

181

People who manage their grief ask questions like these: "How can I rebuild my life?" "How can my friends support me through this transition?" "What can I do next to face reality?" Those in the Victim Trap, however, ask self-defeating questions that keep them from moving forward. For example, they may ask questions like these: "How can I live without her?" "Why did this happen to me?" "What's the use?" Some become so entrenched in their pain that they become clinically depressed.

Depression is different from grief, although both are painful and can feel equally sad. When we grieve effectively, tears or talking help relieve the pain. After a good cry or telling a friend or therapist about our sadness, we feel better. Talking and crying hurts, but we are glad we did it. This is not to imply that one conversation or one tearful experience puts an end to all the pain. Grieving takes time, and the sadness comes upon us like waves on the shore. Sometimes the pain subsides, and then, seemingly out of the blue, we are immersed again in the feelings of loss. But each time we cry or talk or pray or embrace the pain, we let go a little more and our pain decreases.

When someone is depressed, however, nothing seems to help. The tears keep flowing but the sadness never subsides. The sad story is told and retold, but no relief is experienced. Nothing anyone does or says makes any difference.

Melinda mismanaged her grief about her date-rape by slowly sinking into depression. The first signs were an erosion of her self-confidence on the job. She lost her appetite, couldn't sleep through the night, and found it hard to concentrate on what people were saying to her. Rather than get the help she needed, Melinda got stuck in the pain. She missed days of work due to migraine headaches and infections, withdrew from her friends, especially men, and slept away her weekends. Eventually Melinda was asked to leave her practice because of poor job performance. No one could figure out what had happened to such a promising young lawyer. Consumed by her pain, Melinda lost all hope in herself and in the kindness of others.

Katrina became depressed by holding onto her grief as a misguided way to hold onto Martin. No longer able to assess reality, Katrina underestimated the seriousness of her depression and avoided getting professional help.

When we try to avoid grief or get stuck in the sadness, our bodies are dramatically affected. In fact, the chemical makeup of our brains is altered. From research on animals, Jay M. Weiss asserts: "Depressed behavior often can be perpetuated in a vicious circle: the inability to cope alters neural biochemistry, which further accentuates depression, increasing the inability to cope, which further alters neural chemistry, and so on."[1]

Mismanaged grief can lead to a serious chemical imbalance in the brain. Clinical depression shows itself in a number of ways. A clinically depressed person's appetite can change so that weight is lost or gained rapidly. Losing interest in things once enjoyed, a depressed individual develops feelings of worthlessness and inappropriate guilt. One's ability to concentrate or think clearly is limited and physical movements actually slow down or become "shaky." If these feelings go on for a while, the sense of "not caring anymore" can set in, even to the point of having suicidal thoughts. This may not necessarily mean that the person wants to follow through on these impulses, but the thoughts may come anyway.

Professional help is needed if clinical depression sets in as a result of mismanaging grief. Tremendous advances have been made in recent years in the treatment of depression, and no one needs to try to fight through it alone. Severe depression cannot be talked through with a friend but can

183

usually be treated successfully with some combination of therapy and antidepressant medication.

Determining whether we are feeling grief or depression is an important distinction. Since the mismanagement of grief can look like clinical depression, it can be hard to tell the difference. It is even possible for both to be taking place at the same time. If ever in doubt, it is wise to get a second opinion. Rather that make your own diagnosis of the situation, encourage the grieving person in your life to make an appointment with a therapist to get a professional opinion, especially if she or he is having suicidal thoughts. It is your personal responsibility to recognize the limits of your ability to free someone from clinical depression. The best thing you can do is to help them get the professional assistance they need.

Mismanaged Grief Underestimates the Damage Caused
When we mismanage grief we not only perpetrate hurt on ourselves, but on others as well. When we conclude we are powerless, we open the door to devaluing ourselves as human beings at the same time as we blame others. What impact can we have on others when we know deep inside we are weak and incompetent? How can we compete professionally or personally when we are, in fact, defective failures? When we mismanage grief, perpetual sadness replaces hopeful anticipation, a sense of worthlessness replaces self-confidence.

Deep inside Katrina's heart was the fear that Martin left her because she wasn't worthy of his love. In fact, any time Martin did something upsetting to Katrina, she "knew" it was because she wasn't good enough for him. Actually, she was a good match for Martin in every way. They were intellectually, socially, and spiritually compatible. One of the things that undermined their bond, however, was Katrina's belief that she was inadequate.

184

This belief developed many years before she met Martin. As a little girl she thought her father left her waiting at the school yard because she was a bother, much less important than his business meetings or projects. She hugged her knees to comfort herself as she took responsibility for the abusive way her father treated her. There were many reasons her father failed to live up to his parenting responsibilities, all having to do with his own emotional woundedness, but none of these had anything to do with Katrina's worth as a person. Katrina drew an inaccurate conclusion from her father's abusive behavior that affected all of her relationships from that day forward. Mismanaging her grief led her to despairing conclusions about herself and undermined her ability to attach successfully with those she loved.

We often mistreat others in the same way we felt mistreated. Blinded by the tears in our eyes, we do not see that our mismanaged grief damages those around us. Consumed by our own pain, it is impossible for us to imagine that others may also have their own concerns and crises. Furthermore, when in the Victim Trap, we rarely recognize the direct abuse we inflict on those around us.

In her grief, Katrina treated Mara with the same disrespect she felt for herself. Secretly fearing that she was not as good as Mara, Katrina criticized Mara for having the love of a husband and rejected Mara's attempts to make contact. Mara, therefore, began to feel devalued, rejected, and unable to stay connected to her longtime friend.

Katrina had no idea that she was hurting Mara by simultaneously shutting her out and expecting her to respond to her every need. Mara felt she was letting Katrina down, while grieving the loss of her friend. If you are in a relationship with someone mismanaging grief, be on the alert for how you might be hurt. Chances are you are expected to drop everything to respond to the pain while being negated as a

185

person with needs in your own right. If you are unable to give everything this person needs, you will be blamed.

WHY DO WE MISMANAGE OUR GRIEF?

Most of us enjoy periods of solitude to rejuvenate or be creative. But no one enjoys feeling abandoned, left out, or lonely. We grieve when we are confronted, against our will, with the pain of loneliness. We all respond to loneliness in different ways. To some, loneliness is terrifying. Others become confused or disoriented when forced into this kind of isolation. Some of us grow agitated, frustrated, or angry. We all feel pain and react in some way when we lose the human contact we need.

We fall into the Victim Trap when, rather than accept the inevitable human experience of loneliness and learn to cope with it effectively, we grieve and cry and try to push the painful reality away. Anything, it seems, is better than facing the fact that someone or something has moved away from us: a close friend has died and will never be seen again, the marriage is over and cannot be revived, childhood innocence was violated with sexual abuse and cannot be regained, physical illness has resulted in a permanent loss of vitality. We ineffectively grieve what we have yet to accept as real.

What we fail to do in these distressing times is to distinguish between aloneness and loneliness. Aloneness is being apart from others, the temporary breaks we take in our relationships. The capacity to be alone is central to the development of a healthy sense of self, and it gives us a greater ability to be with others in a mature and affirming manner. We must be able to do well alone in order to be with others in a healthy way. Aloneness is our time of contemplation that develops our sensitivity to others. Through the better understanding of ourselves in these times we are

186

better able to relate to others when we are not alone. To fear aloneness suggests that our relationships with others are not secure or predictable, and aloneness gets converted into loneliness.

By contrast, loneliness is when we feel dejected by the awareness of being alone. We feel sad, melancholic, and weighed down as the meaning of being alone changes from constructive contemplation to a painful, downhearted experience of rejection. When we feel lonely we cannot maintain a peaceful solitude so that alone times contribute positively to our life. Instead, we define ourselves as separate from the world.

A good example of this is Rebecca. She was raised in a conservative midwestern family that was very concerned about their appearance in the community. She always dressed neatly, behaved properly, and never made disturbances that might make her stand out from the crowd. Embarrassing her family would have been the worst thing she could have done. Even though she married a good-looking, well-respected man in the community, she was never really happy with her life. Although everyone envied Rebecca, no one really knew her because she never let them in. Growing up so concerned about appearances left Rebecca with the feeling that who she was inside was never good enough. She was afraid to share her true feelings with anyone because she was sure she'd be rejected. Therefore, she felt lonely all the time. It didn't matter whether she was in a crowd or home by herself, she felt constantly disconnected from everyone else. Being alone did not provide Rebecca with an opportunity to reflect on how meaningful her relationships were; it only confirmed what she thought was her destiny—a lonely life.

The distinction we make in our minds between aloneness and loneliness is based upon what we have learned from

187

our relationships. Every one of us is born with a deep, natural need to attach to others in loving, secure relationships. If we had parents who were healthy enough to securely attach to us, we will probably have the capacity to bond well with others. If we have experienced relationships that did a "good-enough"[2] job making us feel safe and cared for, then we may develop the belief that someone will be there for us when we need it. Being alone becomes beneficial to us because being with others is a reliable part of our lives.

If, on the other hand, our childhood attachments were insecure or disrupted in some way, we can be troubled by a prevailing sense of loneliness and a trail of dissatisfying relationships throughout our lives. People like Rebecca and Katrina did not develop a secure sense of their relationships, so they felt powerless and frightened by their times alone. In the Victim Trap, being alone feels like abandonment and aloneness quickly leads to loneliness. Rather than enjoying solitude, we feel disconnected most of the time, so the fight against loneliness goes on constantly.

Because Katrina could not depend on her father for a consistent display of love and protection, she developed what is known as an "anxious" attachment style. Her father was unpredictable and unreliable but would come through for her every once in a while. One of Katrina's happiest memories was on her eighth birthday when her father presented her with a tree house he had built for her. She loved to invite her friends to play in her tree house, so she could tell them proudly that her father had made it for her. When she was sad or lonely, she would sit up in the tree house alone, feeling that this was the one place on earth in which she felt she belonged.

As a woman, Katrina unconsciously expected men to disappoint her, so a sense of anxiety and fear pervaded her dating relationships. Once she met Martin, she clung to him, pressuring him constantly for assurance. No matter what he did or said, Martin was unable to relieve Katrina's sense of anxiety. She promised him that once he married her, she would feel secure in his love. Martin was very surprised that Katrina actually became more dependent and untrusting after their wedding.

If he was late from work she would accuse him of having an affair. She looked through his pockets, his drawers, and his desk for evidence of his unfaithfulness. At first he tried to reassure her, but she only became more suspicious. He withdrew emotionally, spending as much time as he could at work. When he came home, Katrina would scream at him, which caused him to withdraw even more. Martin began sleeping more nights on the couch than in his own bed. Finally, Martin withdrew completely, packed his bags, and moved out. Katrina's fear of being abandoned had set the stage for this to happen.

Katrina was stuck in an anxious attachment pattern that kept her from enjoying the love and intimacy available to her. This pattern also kept her from grieving effectively, learning from her mistakes, and moving into a healthier relationship. Katrina continued to live in her anxiety, fretting about Martin, blaming him for leaving her, swearing to herself she would never trust another man because they were all the same: unreliable and selfish. Then she would see the soft sweater Martin had bought her or spray on some perfume he gave her for Christmas and she would sob over the loss of all he had given to her.

Martin, on the other hand, had what is called a "traumatic" attachment style. He was raised by an emotionally expressive mother who overwhelmed Martin with affection one moment and then yelled and hit him the next. As soon as he graduated from high school he left home, grateful to be away from his mother's intrusiveness. Unfortunately, he replicated his childhood by marrying Katrina who also flooded him with affection and then barraged him with criticism and anger. For a while he tried to pretend that the "real" Katrina was sweet and nurturing while the raging Katrina was just a fluke, a passing problem. When Martin was a boy, he coped with his mother's intrusion by withdrawing. He continued to use the same strategy with his wife until he had withdrawn himself right out of the marriage. While living with someone who mismanaged grief, Martin mismanaged his own responses to loss and fell into the Victim Trap himself.

On the surface, it might appear that Martin was effectively handling his loss of Katrina, since he was the one who decided to move out and displayed the least amount of emotion. In fact, many of his colleagues at work were unaware that Martin and Katrina were separated because Martin behaved as he always had: calm, quiet, and focused on his work. Since Martin disliked overt displays of emotion, he was reluctant to feel his own feelings, let alone discuss them or express them. Martin handled his loss by cutting off from his feelings and living his life on "automatic pilot." He refused to file for divorce, which would have forced him to face his loss. But dysfunctional coping strategies always result in what we are most trying to avoid. In his effort to avoid pain and loneliness, Martin put himself in limbo, unable to realistically address the problems between himself and Katrina while not fully free to move on to a healthier relationship. Martin's powerlessness set him up for the trap.

Whether insecure attachments are between parent and child, friends, or lovers, they result in more woundedness and pain. Ironically, it is harder to grieve "insecure" relationships than those in which the bonds are strong and healthy. This is because relationships with secure attachments produce healthy self-esteem. Combining appropriate boundaries with genuine compassion affirms our self-worth in ways that encourage our separateness from each other while making us feel connected. Individuality becomes a good thing in these kinds of relationships and we are able to be alone from time to time. We know if we start to feel lonely our presence will be welcomed at any time. This sense of separateness-in-relationship grows out of secure attachments in which there is no need for too much closeness or too much distance, a need that always comes from some deeper feelings of insecurity. In this environment we develop the self-esteem to see ourselves as separate from each other but still intimately connected. We are not the same person as the other but we would not be the same person we are now without him or her.

The result of losing someone with whom we have had a secure attachment is healthy grief. We can allow the grief process to take its course because we realize that our feelings are a reaction to the loss of love, not an attempt to keep it alive. We grieve because we have lost something important to us but separate from us.

When we lose a relationship in which our attachment was insecure we feel unfinished, as if we're still trying to get clear on what we needed from the other person. Accepting that the relationship is over is too distressing to admit because we'd have to accept the fact that we'll never get what we need from this person. So the grief process drags on and on. People grieving insecure attachments need a lot of support, sometimes even professional therapy, to avoid falling into the Victim Trap and mismanaging their grief. If they never developed the self-esteem required to deal with difficult emotions, they will have difficulty grieving a complex loss.

HOW TO DEAL WITH THOSE
WHO MISMANAGE THEIR GRIEF

Most of us react to people who are grieving with compassion and sympathy. If, however, they see themselves as powerless,

191

getting close may be hurtful to us and frustrating to them.

When we see someone who is sad or grieving, a natural response is to try to provide comfort for them. In the Victim Trap, however, people are unable to make use of support because to do so would require them to acknowledge their personal power to give and receive help. They simultaneously reject the assistance we offer while asking for more from us. We can easily become confused by those who act dependent upon us while undermining anything positive we attempt to do. Until they are aware of their own ability to successfully grieve their losses and make use of support from others, nothing we can do will ease their pain or confirm that we are being helpful.

The way people in the Victim Trap respond to our support can undermine our sense of self-esteem. Since our attempts to comfort repeatedly fail, it's natural to conclude that the failure is our responsibility. If you're trying to comfort someone in the Victim Trap, you might find yourself asking, "Why can't I be more sensitive?" "How can I say the right words to cheer them up?" or "If I were smarter, I'd know what to do." Be aware of feelings of powerlessness. People in pain need you, which can be a source of positive self-regard if they receive your help. But if you pretend that you can help everyone, especially those in the Victim Trap, you'll soon feel powerless and defeated.

So how can you avoid slipping into the trap? How can you relate to someone mismanaging grief while, at the same time, keep from being pulled into their helplessness? To do this, you must have realistic expectations for them and yourself.

First, *have a realistic understanding of why people in the Victim Trap behave the way they do*. Expect them to be excessively demanding or to shut you out. Some switch between these extremes, overwhelming you with their neediness at one moment and disappearing the next. Recognizing that some feel powerless in their grief will help you predict ways they may try to hurt you and take you off guard. If you identify with Martin, you may need additional distance from those in the Victim Trap, since you will be perceived as the source of the pain and you'll be especially tempted to fall in yourself. If you feel more like Mara, then expect to be blamed sporadically and irrationally.

Second, *be kind to yourself and give yourself time to sort things through, feel your emotions, and heal.* Grief over the loss of closeness in a relationship, even a painful one, is unavoidable. Even if the person mismanaging grief remains in your life, you will have to grieve over the fact that he or she is not available to you the way you wish. Rather than being alarmed by grief, try to see it as evidence that you can love.

We grieve because things matter to us. Grieving is saying goodbye to the meaningful parts of our past. Sometimes it is not a person, but our innocence, peace of mind, financial security, or physical health that we must grieve. We can grieve the loss of our dreams or what could have been that never happened. Grieving the loss of something we never had is sometimes extremely important to do. The point is, grieving is not just "getting over it," but opening the door to creative changes in our lives. We grieve in order to move on. We must make space in our hearts for the new by letting go of the old.

Third, *have reasonable expectations of others in your life*. They will not be able to take your pain away. No one can grieve your losses for you. But others can be with you in your pain. Open yourself up to additional support, invest in relationships that are secure and healthy, and let others care about you as you're changing the way you operate with the grieving people in your life.

Manage Your Grief, Face Your Loneliness

Probably the most famous researcher to study grief is Elizabeth Kubler-Ross.[3] From years of clinical observation and conversations with hundreds of people experiencing loss, she identified a pattern or process of grieving with five stages: denial, anger, bargaining, depression, and acceptance. Not everyone goes through all of the stages in order, and once someone passes through a stage it does not mean he or she may not go back and experience it again. But people in grief, in one form or another, generally go through these five stages.

Grief is a process. It is not a single emotion felt for a moment and then forgotten. Grief requires emotional work that moves us from one stage to the next as we come closer to being able to accept our loss. This is not to say that once we have grieved we will never have to grieve again. But if we do our grief work, it changes us. The holes in our hearts begin to heal when we honestly grieve.

Managing the grief process is hard enough in itself, but what if we don't want to accept a particular loss? This was Katrina's problem. The end product of doing grief work is acceptance. This is exactly where Katrina did not want to go. By refusing to accept the loss of Martin, Katrina refused to let her grief come to an end. As long as she still grieved, she did not have to admit that the relationship with Martin was over. Staying stuck in the sadness somehow kept the hope of a relationship with Martin alive. She felt powerless to go back and powerless to go on, so she became entangled in her grief.

As a result, the natural process of grief over a significant loss became repressed. Katrina did not want to consciously admit to herself that she was working through an emotional process of letting Martin go. She felt unfinished, and her history of an insecure attachment with Martin left

194

her with a dread of the loneliness that was sure to come. Not wanting to face what she was feeling, her unconscious grieving process would show itself from time to time as anger, depression, denial, and futile negotiations with God that she never understood. Never facing any of these feelings as a part of her grief, Katrina felt confused and victimized by her own emotions. She continued to interpret her pain as evidence that she and Martin should be together, rather than seeing it as a part of the process of their coming apart.

All Katrina knew was that something was very wrong. Like Katrina, those in the Victim Trap who do not feel confident about dealing with their emotions often misinterpret their grief. The stages of grief do not feel good when we are working through them. But just because they do not feel good does not mean that something good is not going on. Because Katrina felt bad, she thought ending the relationship with Martin was a bad thing and wrong for her to do. She misinterpreted her grief as a sign that she should go back to the way things were instead of as a door to something completely new.

To avoid falling into the Victim Trap, it is important to face your own sense of loss while retaining your power. Mara needed to recognize that, for the time being, Katrina was not available to her as she had been in the past. Mara's challenge was to grieve this loss in a different way than Katrina was grieving hers. It was tempting for Mara to see herself as powerless, since Katrina withdrew herself from the relationship against Mara's wishes. However, Mara was able to see that Katrina was mismanaging her emotions and she took a different path than her best friend.

Embracing her personal power, Mara made the decision to get help for herself. She joined a women's support group, so that she would have a new place to share her pain. As a consequence, she met other women who were growing in healthy ways, and new friendships emerged. None of the new friendships could replace the long friendship Mara shared with Katrina. Nor did Mara want to abandon Katrina during this time. Instead, Mara's new relationships gave her added strength to remain in the relationship with Katrina. The support group helped Mara discern which, if any, of Katrina's criticisms were accurate and how best to care for Katrina while she was ensnared in her mismanaged grief.

Facing loss effectively can take different forms. Like Mara, you may want to join a support group and discuss your losses. If the person mismanaging grief is especially dangerous to your sense of power, a therapist may give you the individualized attention you need. Keeping contact with other friends and family members is important to help with reality testing. And be sure to give yourself time to feel sad, take things slowly, and grieve the loss.

Those in the Victim Trap often make the mistake of trying to get all of their attachment needs met in one place. Don't fall into this trap yourself. While the fulfilling relationship you grieve is irreplaceable, you can use your power to build other supportive, secure relationships to help make the loss more bearable.

The willingness to accept losses lays the groundwork for healing. The ability to embrace aloneness opens the door to intimacy and connection. The paradox of healing, we believe, is the spiritual principle of death and resurrection. We must first experience the death—the loss, the sadness, the aloneness—before we can enjoy the newness of rebirth.

Most of us long for rebirth but would rather forgo the death portion of this process. In the death process, we feel betrayed, confused, angry, sad. Like the famous words of Jesus on the cross, we cry out, "My God, my God, why have you forsaken me?"[4] Why have we been so utterly abandoned at the time when we are most in need of protection or comfort? Managing grief involves asking these painful questions of God and of those who claim to love us, whether we like the answers we receive or not.

And then we wait. We wait for the healing that comes not from ourselves but from the love of others. While most of us would prefer to ignore this profound dependence, the fact remains that none of us heals or is reborn outside relationship. We need others and, at times, we must wait for the transformation.

We are not idle while we wait, however. We cry our tears, ask the questions burning in our souls, and face our loneliness. We wonder what we did to deserve such horrible treatment or tragic losses. We reevaluate the way we thought the world worked and come up with what M. Scott Peck refers to as "new maps" of reality.[5] And eventually, resurrection occurs for us—usually slowly, and usually when we are looking the other way.

To manage our grief, we must decide to face our loneliness. Making this decision begins the process of transformation from dejection to healing, from isolation to love. It is especially difficult to face our loneliness in a society that overvalues individualism. Nietzsche established a value for our culture when he said, "The strongest man is the loneliest man."[6] We have been told since childhood that it is "lonely at the top," meaning we should not make connection to others important if we expect to succeed. Facing loneliness as an experience to be transformed becomes counterproductive in a society that worships individuality. Living with loneliness has been our model. Think of the American heroes we have been led to emulate: Benjamin Franklin, Davy Crockett, John Wayne, and Henry David Thoreau on Walden Pond. Family life and connection to others only got in their way of pursuing the American dream.

197

This kind of modeling has resulted in a society composed of a "Lonely Crowd."[7] Here people are more focused on achievement than intimacy and almost completely unable to grieve their losses because attachments to others weren't supposed to matter in the first place. In America, many of us have forgotten that "the opposite of loneliness is not togetherness, but intimacy."[8]

It is not being alone but the fear of it that is the problem. Transforming loneliness into something constructive in our lives requires us to understand ourselves and have the capacity to tolerate difficult emotions. Transforming loneliness has nothing to do with being around other people, or even getting one to commit to be there for life. It has everything to do with self-perception. The clinging, dependent person is always around other people but always lonely, even in a crowd. Developing the ability to form secure attachments and a self-image that enables us to see relationships as opportunities for loving, supportive exchanges is the basis for transforming loneliness. It is not what we get but what we have to give that makes the difference. Love must flow outward or it dies. If we become too afraid of loneliness and act too quickly to defend ourselves from it, we can panic and make the mistake of trying to cure ourselves of loneliness. When loneliness becomes linked with fear, we lose our ability to make secure attachments.

Learn from the Past, Stay in the Present
Facing your current loss will give you an opportunity to assess your relationships in general. If you have secure and healthy attachments with people, the grieving process is often less difficult than if your relationships are unstable or insecure. Take this opportunity to strengthen all your relationships, especially those that are the most important to you. Even if you weren't raised in a family with secure

198

attachments, it's never too late to develop healthier, more empowered relationships in your life.

For example, Janis grew up in a family with insecure attachments. She was emotionally neglected by her parents and brothers. Her family valued boys over girls and she was left out of many of the family activities, such as sports, hunting, and fishing. She grew up to be a lonely woman with few friends and an inability to control her eating. Her doctor warned her that if she did not get into some type of treatment program she would die an early death due to obesity.

Janis started attending Overeaters Anonymous and met several women who shared her pain. After a couple of years of attending OA, she also started seeing a therapist who helped her look at the neglect in her childhood. Janis and her therapist bonded deeply and securely, giving Janis an experience of healthy love. Her relationships with her therapist and the women in her support group gave her what she had always needed: people who attended to her and let her have meaning in their lives.

Janis tried to make contact with her family, but her parents and brothers were still unavailable to her. So she reached out to her grandmother, who was quite elderly at this time. The rest of the family were busy with their lives and did not have time for Grandma. During the last two years of her grandmother's life, Janis visited her every weekend at the convalescent home where she lived. Each week they talked about the past and worked through misunderstandings. Janis and her grandmother bonded deeply.

One morning Janis received a phone call from the hospital saying her grandmother had had a stroke. She drove to the hospital and stayed with her all night, telling her grandmother that she loved her. Her grandmother never regained consciousness and died the next day. Even though she felt terribly sad, Janis was comforted by the fact that she and her grandmother had said all there was to say. She knew her grandmother was secure in her love and she had no regrets. Janis still misses her grandmother, but her grief is clean and bearable.

Her healthy attachment to her grandmother was so strong that even though they are separated by death, Janis often feels her grandmother close. She wears her grandmother's jewelry, not with sadness but with pride, and often tells her friends stories about her grandmother. Because Janis had a secure attachment to her grandmother, their relationship allowed them both to be very separate people even though they were emotionally intimate. This made their separation by her grandmother's death easier to bear.

Janis escaped the Victim Trap when she found the personal power to reach out and develop secure attachments in her world. Not everyone in her family wanted to respond to her offer of a healthy, mutual relationship, but her grandmother did. Through her therapy, support group, and her relationship with her grandmother, Janis learned that she could have relationships in which she was valued.

Take Responsibility and Hold Others Accountable

As is true with anyone in the Victim Trap, those mismanaging grief blame others for their losses. They will blame you for things you've never done, for things they think you should have done, or for feelings they don't want to own. Since the blame is often accompanied with tears and emotional intensity, you can become severely confused and have your self-esteem damaged.

Remember, give little credence to the criticisms of those mismanaging grief, knowing that their perceptions are motivated by intense pain and they may attempt to relieve their suffering by blaming you. Knowing this may help you feel compassion for them, but don't let your compassion cause you to underestimate the danger of this misguided energy. Grief is a powerful emotion, as powerful as fear or anger or any other feeling. When people mismanage their grief, the intensity of their repressed power can harm you in addition to themselves.

Also, as time goes on, people in the Victim Trap want to be supported in the same way they were when their crisis or loss first occurred. It is natural to expect, after a period of time, the pain to decrease and the loss to be accepted. Since those who mismanage their grief do not want or know how to complete their grief, they will expect to be attended to indefinitely. If you find yourself falling into the Victim Trap, hold firmly to your own reality, gaining strength from your support system. Be clear about what you are willing to give and what you are not. Remember, no matter how much you give to those in the Victim Trap, it will never be enough. You don't have the power to eliminate their pain or rescue them.

For example, Katrina gave up her power by becoming entrenched in her grief. She could only imagine one solution to her loneliness. Because Martin meant "everything" to her, she felt like she was nothing without him. Her unrelenting grief became a defense against a loneliness she could not face because she had given all of the power for her healing to someone else—and he was gone.

Mara was pulled into the trap, feeling as powerless and helpless as Katrina felt. Mara needed to embrace her personal power, recognizing that she could not "make" everything better for Katrina. If you're in Mara's situation, you can take care of yourself by making sure you take time for yourself. This is especially important if those in the Victim Trap demand continual attention from you. Use your support system to give you the stamina to withstand the inevitable criticisms. Even if others aren't ready to let their

201

lives stabilize, put effort into making your life as enjoyable as possible. Do things you like to do. Plan ahead so you have something to look forward to each day. Exercise, eat well, and get plenty of rest. You may even be going through your own grieving process as well as having to deal with the emotional assaults of someone mismanaging grief.

PERSONAL REFLECTION

To describe the mismanagement of grief as a protracted experience that seems to have no end is not to say that the management of grief is a brief process that should be accomplished in any specific period of time. The question is not how long it takes to grieve, but *why* we are grieving. Are we grieving in order to reach a place of acceptance of our loss? Each time we let ourselves feel, talk, and cry about our loss, do we feel a little bit closer to that goal? Or are we grieving to avoid loneliness, letting our grief keep us attached to someone we have actually lost?

The answers to these questions are not always clear. Consider something over which you're grieving. To understand how to deal with someone mismanaging grief, it is good to consider how to deal with grief in your own life. It is not really possible to understand the depths of someone else's sorrow until you have understood the depths of your own.

What does this remind me of? Most of the experiences that are most painful in adulthood are those we recognize as similar, consciously or unconsciously, to trauma or neglect from childhood. While Katrina was extremely sad over the loss of Martin, her pain was greatly intensified because this event reminded her of a pattern of parental abandonment she suffered as a child. As a child, she was indeed dependent upon her father for her very survival. The fear was real and powerful for her.

However, her loss of Martin was not a threat to her survival. She lost a great many things when Martin left, but these things were separate from the things she lost in relationship to her father. Had Katrina chosen to grieve the pain of her past separately from her current loss, she would have been able to manage her pain and have more realistic expectations for herself in the future.

Do you feel sadness or loneliness that nothing seems to soothe? Maybe a past trauma has been triggered unconsciously through this current situation and you need to explore the past so you can heal in the present. Were you insecurely attached to a parent or someone important through neglect, intrusiveness, or a combination of the two?

What feelings am I experiencing now? Having explored the power of our past experiences, we are free to feel our current emotions. While overwhelming feelings often come from childhood loss, losses in the present are easier to contain. What are the real feelings you are experiencing in the here and now? Are you feeling sadness, anger, a sense of betrayal, regret, or guilt?

What feelings are underneath what I am experiencing now? Once you identify the most obvious feelings of grief, spend some time looking beneath the surface of your pain. Katrina felt clingy and helpless, but underneath those feelings she had a sense of loneliness she had never wanted to face. Mara, on the other hand, felt frustrated and irritated. Underneath those feelings were a desire for closeness and feelings of rejection. Usually our feelings are layered, and the more we explore, the closer we come to our core needs and longings.

How can I best express my feelings to maximize healing and growth? When we operate from insecurity, we usually destroy what we hope to achieve. Katrina and Martin both wanted a healthy, loving marriage, but their insecure attachment undermined their ability to create security. Has this been true in your life? As you grieve the loss of a parent, a lover, a friend, or someone else who has hurt you, do you find that you sabotage what you are trying to achieve?

Katrina could have made a difference in her friendship with Mara by facing the truth about her feelings of loneliness. Instead of accusing Mara of being intrusive, she could have told her about her fears and her needs. Rather than withdrawing from emotional confrontation, Mara could have insisted that Katrina get professional help to express her needs for connection and tolerate her aloneness.

How can you best express your genuine feelings? What may come naturally to you may be what undermines your grieving process and gets you stuck. Be creative. Ask for help. Find new ways to express yourself.

How can I hold those who hurt me accountable for their actions? Katrina first needed to hold her parents accountable for the pain of her childhood. This does not mean that Katrina or Martin should blame their parents for their failed marriage. It is not their parents' fault that the connection between Katrina and Martin was damaged. Katrina's father is responsible, however, for being emotionally unpredictable and unavailable to her on a regular basis. Martin's mother is responsible for violating his emotional boundaries and for her physical abuse. Both Martin and Katrina needed to face these realities within themselves, and perhaps with their parents, and specifically identify how amends could be made.

In addition to holding their parents accountable, Katrina and Martin needed to hold each other accountable for the mutual hurt they caused each other. Mara needed to hold Katrina accountable for her behavior in their friendship.

Who has hurt you? What specifically occurred? How

204

can amends be made between you? How can you set boundaries in relationships that will make for more secure attachments? Who do you need to set limits with to minimize the
insecurity in your life?

What is my responsibility in creating this situation?
As children we have minimal power to respond to or protect ourselves from abuse. As you deal with childhood
issues, it is important to accurately assess your true responsibility, which would naturally increase with your age and
power. It is our observation that children tend to take much
more responsibility than is warranted, while adults tend to
minimize their responsibility. Either way, even if it is not
your fault that you turned out the way you did, it is your
responsibility if you stay that way.

Look realistically at your current loss. What did you do
in the past to contribute to this situation? How have you
sabotaged your attempts at secure attachment? How did
you intensify the situation? In what ways have you under-
utilized your power and left yourself open to hurt and loss?

Now, look realistically at what you have gained. What
can you be grateful for so you can move on? How can you
responsibly acknowledge the past without clinging to it?
Can you say it was good and say goodbye, at the same time?
It was not all bad then, and you are not bad now for coming to accept this loss.

What can I learn from this situation? No experience
is a failure if we learn something. Katrina and Mara, while
in the middle of extremely painful losses, have the opportunity to make needed changes and bring healthy love into
their lives.

How have childhood experiences limited your ability to
love and enjoy life in the present? How have the losses of
your childhood damaged your ability to grieve effectively?
Are you holding onto the pain as a way to hold onto a

relationship or situation that is no longer healthy for you?

It is important to take the lessons, especially the painful ones, and use this information in the future so that a similar situation need not happen again. As you grieve the loss, embrace the lesson and prepare to move into a more loving, secure future.

How am I powerful in the situation? Realistically, what are your strengths now? You are probably expending a tremendous amount of energy if you are mismanaging your grief or trying to love someone who is. The fear of loneliness that underlies it is only soaking up even more emotional energy that could be used elsewhere. Moving beyond denial, the first stage of grief, may threaten to throw you into a black hole that will drain you of your ability to function. But the truth is, managing grief takes you to the end of a process where you will feel empowered to love in deeper ways than you could have before.

Is someone you know blinded to the needs and feelings of people around him or her because of grief? What resources are available that might help either of you? Are you hurting those who love you in any way because you are consumed with your own grief?

How can I redefine the relationship? This is one of the most important questions Mara needed to ask herself about Katrina. Because Katrina saw Martin as the key to her happiness, she placed him in a role he could never fulfill and destined herself for disappointment in her relationship with him and with others. Is there a similar relationship in your life that you need to redefine? Mara needed to maintain her personal power by holding Katrina accountable for her behavior in their friendship. Rather than cutting off the relationship, which would not have resolved the loneliness, Mara needed to redefine it so they could still have each other in their lives.

Do you have a similar situation in your life that needs your attention? Perhaps there is someone you're grieving over in a way that never seems to help. Even if this person is out of your life, how can you redefine the relationship you carry around in your head? How do you need to see him or her and yourself differently? Who can you talk to about this that might have a helpful perspective?

Are you grieving the loss of some aspect of your life such as your reputation, innocence, financial security, or childhood? Then perhaps you need to redefine your relationship to yourself. Do you have a self-soothing presence when you are alone, or are you critical of yourself? What is your self-talk like? When you are alone with you, what is it like? How can you learn to become a better friend to yourself in your times of need? Would you say to a friend the things you say to yourself?

NOTES
1. J. M. Weiss, "Psychological Factors in Stress and Disease," *Scientific American*, June 1972, p. 79-87.
2. D. W. Winnicott, *The Maturational Process and the Facilitating Environment* (New York: International University Press, 1965), p. 145.
3. Elisabeth Kubler-Ross has written many books on the subject of grief. For more information, we suggest your begin with *On Death and Dying* (New York: Macmillan, 1969).
4. Mark 15:34 from the *New Revised Standard Version*, copyright 1989, by the Division of Christian Education of the National Council of the Churches of Christ in the USA, used by permission, all rights reserved.
5. M. Scott Peck, MD, *The Road Less Traveled* (New York: Simon & Schuster, 1978), pp. 44-51.
6. Friedrich Nietzsche, who also said, "Help thyself: then everyone will help thee, too," in *Twilight of the Idols* (New York: Penguin Books, 1968), p. 23.
7. David Reisman with Nathan Glazer and Reuel Denney, *The Lonely Crowd* (New Haven: Yale University Press, 1961).
8. Richard Bach, *Running from Safety: An Adventure of the Spirit* (New York: Morrow, 1994), p. 67.

WHO'S
TO BLAME?

WHO'S TO BLAME for life's pain? The answer to this question is no one. Paradoxically, we are all responsible. We're each responsible for our personal happiness, for our choices that have negative consequences on others and for claiming our personal power.

We have the chance to take responsibility for ourselves in each and every one of our relationships. Relationships challenge us to grow by putting us into new situations while giving us the opportunity to face old self-defeating patterns once again. In fact, we believe that one of the main purposes of relationships is to give us the opportunity to heal from past wounds by bringing new love and acceptance into our lives.

Since none of us has come through life without some wounds and bruises, every relationship involves people who have been victimized to some degree or other. Consequently, there are no perfect people out there somewhere with whom we can create the ideal relationship. We can, however, assess our relationships according to their degree of health or dysfunction, investing our efforts in creating the healthiest situations possible for ourselves.

The following chart outlines the continuum between healthy relationships and those who are caught in the Victim Trap:

Victim Trap Belief System Versus Personal Power Perspective

Stability:	Chronic crises and transition	Stable with episodic crises
Personal Power:	Blames self and others	Holds self and others accountable
Sense of Reality:	Unstable, isolated	Flexible and shared reality
Identity:	Past abuse	Ongoing successful relationships
Boundaries:	Permeable or overly rigid	Sets and honors them
Capacity for Growth:	Repetitive mistakes	Learns from mistakes
Capacity for Change:	Rigid, closed unrealistic expectations	Open, realistic expectations
Capacity for Resolution:	Clings to others, or premature endings	Finishes, moves on
Capacity to Manage Emotions:	Overwhelmed, controlled by mismanaged feelings	Wide range of conscious emotion, well-managed
Capacity to Forgive:	Excuses or seeks revenge	Forgives and remembers

A word of caution is in order before using this model to assess your relationships. Like all models, it falls short of encompassing life's complexities. Be careful not to use this model to blame yourself or anyone else. Blaming will accomplish nothing other than pulling your relationships further into the Victim Trap. Rather than view this chart as an either-or assessment about your relationships, we suggest that you see these characteristics as two opposite extremes

210

on a continuum, with your relationship most likely falling somewhere in the middle. The further out your relationship falls on the continuum, the healthier or more entrapped it is likely to be.

STABILITY

We believe it is hard, if not impossible, to tell at first meeting if a relationship will fall into the Victim Trap. This is especially true if the relationship begins with one or both parties experiencing some kind of crisis or transition such as divorce, death of a loved one, job change, graduation, or retirement. In any crisis, we all need space to flounder and find new footing, along with additional support through this process. So how do we know if we're genuinely supporting someone or unintentionally disempowering him or her and pushing this relationship into the Victim Trap?

How we feel when we're in the relationship is an excellent indicator. A relationship with someone who is genuinely growing and changing will inspire us, excite us, and give back to us. Even in situations where enormous effort is asked of us, we feel rewarded when those we love succeed and accomplish their goals. In some cases, it may take many years before a person achieves the healing desired. In fact, when someone has been physically or mentally disabled through an accident or abuse, independent functioning may never be completely desirable or possible. But when these people are acting from a position of personal power, our investment feels worthwhile.

When we invest in relationships caught in the Victim Trap, on the other hand, we feel ripped off. We listen and feel unheard. We make suggestions and hear "Yes, *but* I can't because. . . ." The degree of frustration and powerlessness we may feel is not dependent on the duration of the relationship but on the degree of powerlessness the other person brings to the relationship.

If you think your relationship might be slipping into the Victim Trap, ask yourself questions such as these: "Have I expected to see change before now and been repeatedly disappointed?" "Do I keep changing the time frame of my expectations to accommodate my disappointment?" "Do I make excuses for the other person?" If the answer is "yes," the relationship may be in serious trouble.

PERSONAL POWER

How is power managed in your relationship? In healthy, healing relationships you and your partner feel mutually powerful. The healthier the relationship, the more we are able to "do business" with another empowered person. People who are confident of their personal power listen to us express our feelings and then share with us how they feel.

Destructive relationships, on the other hand, occur between people who mismanage their power, feeling either overly responsible or powerless to cope with life's stresses. The more a relationship is caught in the Victim Trap, the more dangerous, disempowering, and distressing it will be. The more you talk, the less you are heard and the more confusing your relationship seems to become. Like struggling in quicksand, the more you try to break free, the further you sink into confusion and darkness.

In relationships where power is shared, both parties are supported in their individual and shared goals. This is not true if one or both of the parties relates from a perspective of personal powerlessness. Even if you try to assert your own power, relating to someone who believes he or she is powerless usually results in your feeling defeated and frustrated. If you are investing energy in a relationship with someone who functions with the Victim Trap belief system, you are caught in the Victim Trap whether you realize it or not. It is unlikely that you will find happiness in this relationship.

A major obstacle to pulling a relationship out of the Victim Trap is that by pointing out that one or both of you feel powerless, your partner may retreat or feel overcome by shame. Your attempts to become more conscious about the problems in the relationship may be experienced by your partner as criticism. Not surprisingly, your partner may feel powerless to do anything about the problem, triggering an outburst of blaming.

The Victim Trap belief system divides people into two categories: "good" or "bad," "us" or "them," "dangerous" or "safe." If you challenge this belief when a person is not ready to let it go, you will probably be moved into the bad, them, dangerous categories. Prepare for this possibility and protect yourself from taking their accusations too seriously. While we all need to be open to hearing how we have hurt others, when taking on more personal power the feedback we get from those who do not want change is fairly unreliable.

Remember, blaming never helps. Working toward shared power is not a demand but an invitation to a relationship that works for both of you. Emphasize your shared responsibility in creating your relationship. Your goal is not to find someone to blame but to take responsibility for yourself.

Your responsibility is to recognize your power in relationships and utilize it to maximize growth. Believing you are powerful enables you to recognize and honor your limitations. Personal power is not about being more than someone else, but about knowing who you are and who you are not. Powerful people are comfortable allowing others to be different from themselves and are free to be vulnerable and strong at the same time.

Putting your focus on responsibility instead of blame

means you are interested in solutions instead of problems, which keeps you constantly engaged in life and in pursuit of peace of mind. How do you feel about your relationship? Do you feel empowered and excited? Challenged and motivated? Or do you feel frustrated and powerless? Disappointed and defeated? You can tell if you are in relationships with truly powerful people if you feel powerful yourself as a result of being around them. True power empowers others.

Personal power often results in a profound sense of peace. Peace is a dynamic way of engaging in life, not the ascetic withdrawal from it. People caught in the Victim Trap never achieve peace in life because they are constantly trying to avoid things. The truth is, the greatest peace does not come from trying to avoid the pain caused by relationships in the past but from dealing with it well in the present. This is the challenge for all of us, and it is the key to freedom from the Victim Trap.

SENSE OF REALITY

If you have ever been in the Victim Trap, at some point you probably began to question if you were in touch with reality. Things you said were used against you, distorted so that you couldn't recognize them; your motives were questioned; at times you were told you were a hurtful person when you were trying to help, and you ended up asking yourself things like, "What am I doing here?" Somehow the relationship challenged who you thought you were.

The healthier the relationship, the easier we can come to agreement about past events and what those events mean. We create a shared reality with those who see themselves as wounded yet personally powerful. A shared reality does not require that both people experience the relationship or life in identical ways. Each person will

214

always have his or her own perspective. But those who share a common reality agree on the major aspects of history, the parameters of the relationship, understand how each partner feels, and accept the similarities and differences between themselves.

Can you both discuss your views and feelings and come to a common understanding? To establish mutual power in the relationship, you must both understand the other's perspective and get to the place where you can honestly say you understand why the other feels the way he or she does. It is not so much agreement as it is understanding that is the sign of a shared reality.

The most difficult part of creating a shared reality can be believing that both parties are mutually powerful. People in the Victim Trap illustrate their immense power by being able to trigger doubts in us about what we feel, what we see, what we've experienced. They are tremendously invested in drawing us into a view of reality in which they are seen as powerless and we are to blame for their pain or their salvation. Do not underestimate the intensity of anyone's ability to influence your sense of reality. In fact, it can feel like a matter of life and death to someone who feels overwhelmed and totally dependent upon you. Be aware that if you find yourself believing it is you and one other person "against the world," you're in deep trouble.

To avoid becoming enmeshed in the Victim Trap, develop a strong, healthy support network. The more people in your network the better. If you have a long-term, intimate relationship with someone who has adopted a powerless perspective, it may be helpful to find a skilled therapist who can help you deal with your partner's blame and mismanaged emotions. Support groups have proven to be very helpful in sorting out these kinds of things. Friends and family members, some who may know both of you personally, and some who may not, can help give you a variety of perspectives and insight.

Expect those relationships caught in the Victim Trap to work against you in developing a support network. You may feel pressure to cut other people out of your life, as the other person strives to isolate you from anyone who could challenge the bond between you. Those caught in the trap unconsciously want to control you and can't if you have strong relationships with others who share a different reality. You may be told to doubt the intentions of others and that you are disloyal or "bad" for talking to anyone else about them. Beware if you find yourself feeling protective of those who try to isolate you like this or defending them against the insight of your support group. This is a clue that you have fallen into the Victim Trap and are no longer coming from a reality that is shared by people who own their personal power.

IDENTITY

The way we view ourselves is constantly changing, modified and altered by each new experience. If our experiences confirm how we see ourselves, then we become all the more convinced of our perspective. However, when we have experiences that contradict our current self-image, often the way we view ourselves changes as well. If an experience is especially traumatic, we can make the mistake of resting our entire identity on how we felt in that particular moment.

When we fall into the Victim Trap, our identities are heavily influenced, if not defined, by past abuse. For example, rather than viewing herself as a personally powerful woman who was temporarily overpowered and raped, a woman may say, "I = the rape." The rape becomes the primary content of her identity. Often this change in self-identity results from the intensity that occurs between the rapist and the victim during the actual offense. The rapist and the woman being raped agree emotionally, at that moment in time, that he is strong and she is weak, he is powerful and she is powerless. Drawing that conclusion, under intense emotional force, can be deeply imprinted in the unconscious.

Similarly, a man who is divorcing may have previously seen himself as a good man, a good provider, a sexy lover, powerful in his own right, able to protect himself from harm. But in the process of divorce, with emotions heightened, cruel words spoken, and the battle of attorneys, he may come to see himself as the powerless victim of his ex-wife and the court system. The supportive words of friends cannot drown out the reality shared by himself, his ex-wife, and the court personnel, which in his mind redefine him as impotent, powerless, and defenseless. When we are overpowered, even if only for a moment, our identities can be changed, sometimes in dramatic ways. Previously competent people can give up, feeling hopeless and convinced that they are no longer powerful people.

To escape the Victim Trap, we must allow a sense of personal power back into our lives as a basis for our identities. To redefine ourselves as powerful, we must change the meaning of the past experiences through which we gave up our power. While we cannot change history, we can change what our past experiences mean to us. However, merely discussing the past won't help if we don't change the way we look at it. We only benefit from examining past abuse if we change both how we view the past and how we view ourselves.

To empower herself, the woman who was raped may change the meaning of the assault from a sexual event to an act of violence, leaving her freer to view herself as innocent of sexual misconduct. She can take pride in how she responded to this violation by telling the truth about the event, getting help, taking a self-defense class, pressing charges against her assailant, or taking other positive actions. Rather than define herself as a rape victim or even a survivor, she can define herself as a woman of courage, with many challenging experiences, one of which was rape.

The man, enraged and blamed for a failed marriage, can change the meaning of this loss from a failure that is solely his fault to a situation in which both parties contributed. By refusing to enter into his ex-wife's negative views of him, he can decide for himself what kind of man he genuinely is. Painful as the divorce may be, this experience can become a positive foundation for his next relationship. Failures can be redefined as beginning points; feelings of powerlessness can be rejected as a foundation for identity and seen as particular experiences, as points in time. Talking about painful events for the purpose of changing what they mean to us can be extremely healing when we feel safe, cared for, and experience a shared reality.

When the meaning of abusive events in our lives changes, so does our self-definition and sense of personal power. The event of being overpowered or taken advantage of does not have to mean that we *equal* powerless. When we reject the views of those who hurt us, we can move into a shared reality with those who love us and see us as personally powerful individuals. In order to have healthy relationships now, we must experience ourselves as powerful and valuable people. Selecting those who will shape our self-image is critical to restoring our personal power.

BOUNDARIES

As we've said previously, one of the best indicators of whether a relationship has fallen into the Victim Trap is how you feel. Are you free to experience happiness and fulfill-ment even if those around you are not? Or are you trying to make others do what you want because that is the only way you can be happy? Have you given over your power to them or have you retained your sense of well-being and ability to make choices? Having the ability to support your loved ones without becoming enmeshed in their feelings indicates that strong, healthy boundaries exist in your relationships.

By applying the three steps of accountability to a rela-tionship, we give ourselves and others the opportunity to set and honor personal boundaries. Again, these three steps are: (1) describe the event or behavior, (2) describe how this event or behavior affected you, and (3) describe how amends could be made to restore the relationship.

While these steps are simple, they are rarely easy to fol-low. When you are in the Victim Trap, things can get messy if you try to set healthy boundaries. Setting a personal boundary can consume a tremendous amount of energy when you are dealing with someone who does not share your reality. When this is the case, it is important to remember that the goal is to get better, not just feel better. It may be a struggle to effect changes in a relationship, but establishing clear boundaries and mutual responsibility is essential.

When setting boundaries becomes difficult, coming to a shared reality with another person may seem impossible. Unresolved pain in relationships acts as a barrier to a shared reality. This is when you need the support of a community of others who can help you. Everyone needs the experience of a shared reality to deal with problems in life. The com-munity you seek should know you well and provide counsel you respect. You will probably need the advice of more than one person, and your counselors may need to be separate from your relationship. Remember that your own pain affects your view of things, so don't remain isolated from those you love and respect as you try to get a clear perspective.

A word of caution is in order about how to best utilize other relationships to help you set boundaries and hold others accountable. Some people, out of their sense of powerlessness, gather around them others who will confirm their perspectives—typically that they have been terribly mistreated and you (and perhaps others) are powerful and guilty of abuse. Those who feel especially powerless will not speak for themselves, hiding behind the comments of others with statements like, "My brother said you had no right to do what you did" or "My therapist said your request was unreasonable and unfair." Nothing is less productive than you and someone else lining up supporters for your conflicting views like two competing generals recruiting soldiers for war. No one is seeking a shared reality in this case, since you are both simply trying to assert that your reality is the only true one that can exist.

Most of us are able to convince another of our views, especially if we distort the facts or omit a few. When we feel in danger or overpowered, a natural response is to find someone who sees things our way. Indeed, we need others to share our reality in order to stabilize and move ahead. But there is a fine line between receiving the support we need to become open to both constructive criticism and affirmation and simply using others to bolster our sagging confidence and distorted thinking. Only you, sometimes through painful honesty, can know if you are relying on others to regain personal power or as a strategy to outmaneuver your "opponent." Careful self-reflection can help you decide if your support network is helping you set appropriate boundaries or if you are using those relationships as weapons against others in your life. Ask yourself if you are really trying to create something better in the relationship, or are you trying to keep from looking at something within yourself?

As you set new boundaries, observing how others respond to this process will reveal their ability or inability to do business with you. Those who can negotiate boundaries and personal space with you are those with whom you are safe. However, those who rigidly hold to their own "reality" and refuse to honor your boundaries are dangerous to you. Those who give up their "reality" easily, replacing their view with yours, are also dangerous. Their respect for your boundaries is only superficial and will not last if you are not around to continually reset them. These people are easily swayed and will change their perspective as soon as they speak with someone else. The safest people are those who retain a flexible but consistent view of their world and whose sense of self is strong enough to maintain their own boundaries.

Consider this example. Your sister calls you often, usually around the time you go to bed, and talks about her problems long into the night. You feel sorry for her because you've always seen her as less intelligent than yourself, and you feel a bit obligated to take care of her. Consequently, for several years now you've put up with losing sleep so you can meet her needs. In other words, you have both agreed to let her play the role of the powerless one in the relationship.

You are now ready to set boundaries that protect your needs and also affirm her personal power. She is, in fact, quite powerful and resourceful. After all, she has for years now convinced you to sacrifice your needs in order to take care of her. That is quite an accomplishment. Realizing that your cooperation in this relationship undermines her self-esteem and violates your privacy, you tell her that you need to make some changes. You say that you love her and want to support her but feel that you've taken on too much responsibility for her life. Also, you need your sleep and want to change the times when the two of you talk. You tell her when you would like to be available and on which days,

221

and that you will be putting the answering machine on after 10:00 p.m. What is her reaction?

Since few of us like change, your sister will probably try to talk you out of this. But as you stand your ground, telling her again how you feel (but not blaming her), she will probably fall into one of two camps: she will respond from the personal power perspective or from the position of the Victim Trap belief system.

If she is drawing you into the Victim Trap, she will most likely respond with blame—either blaming you or herself. She may blame you for no longer caring about her, for abandoning her in a time of need, or for being a lousy sibling. Or she may fall into self-loathing shame and say something like, "I know I'm such a mess. No one wants me around. I don't know how you put up with me for this long." If she responds with blame, she is not responding like someone with whom you can do business. Rather, she is acting like someone from whom you need protection.

On the other hand, she may respond by seeing how this change affirms her personal power. She might say, "I didn't realize this was an imposition for you; I'm sorry and wish I had known earlier. I can see that calling you late at night is hard on you and I won't do it anymore."

In addition, she may say, "I really like hearing about what you need in this relationship. For years it's felt imbalanced, like you do all the giving and I do all the taking. I'm glad to hear how I can be more responsive to you. I hope you let me give to you in more ways in the future."

A powerful person will find other ways to have their needs met if you set boundaries that don't quite fit with their desires. For example, your sister may say, "I like talking at night, even though you no longer want to do that. So I'm going to ask my other friends if any of them like to stay up late and talk. I'll take responsibility for getting my own needs met and call you when it works better for you."

At that point you may feel a twinge of jealousy, imagining your sister confiding in someone else, which would signal that you've unconsciously benefited from this imbalanced relationship. Learn to tolerate such twinges and allow her to grow beyond the confines of your relationship. You will both benefit and experience more personal power as you do.

You can apply this approach to any relationship. Ask yourself these questions:

1. What can I do to protect myself and maximize my future growth?
2. What can I do to maximize the other person's growth?
3. What can I do to create a safe, healthy relationship?

Taking responsibility involves setting boundaries to keep hurtful people at a safe distance and facing whatever feelings we have as a result of being abused. Exerting personal power results in utilizing resources around us and refusing to isolate ourselves with feelings of shame, loneliness, and rejection. Escaping the Victim Trap stops abuse rather than perpetuates it by drawing power from self-love rather than defensive self-protection. People caught in the Victim Trap blame others because they see power as existing somewhere outside of themselves. Those who take responsibility for their pain and their happiness can do so because they see power as existing within.

CAPACITY FOR GROWTH

Everyone engages in relationships that bring up past pain. People choose the familiar, even if it isn't good for them. If you are like the rest of us, you have passed up opportunities for new patterns of relationship because they didn't excite or interest you. Instead, your unconscious selection process directed you to complete unfinished business from the past. The relationships that most excite us are the ones that bring up unconscious feelings, powerful attractions that may mystify even as they trap us. If resolution is achieved, we can move on to healthier patterns of relating. But if not, we can relive the same painful experience over and over again.

Those in the Victim Trap go in circles, using their connection to the past to create more problems to solve with no payoff. Like someone with one foot nailed to the floor, they spend a tremendous amount of energy trying to get away but they always end up in the same place that they started. On the surface, it makes little sense why anyone would participate for very long in a relationship like this, yet many of us have made this mistake more than once. Why is that?

We fall into the Victim Trap because there is something very attractive about it, at least on the surface. When people come to us, needing us, maybe even adoring us, it can be hard to resist their allure. We want to be special, able to help, able to find love in a "bigger than life" sort of way. They may say things like, "I can't make it without you," "I've never met anyone as wonderful (or strong or intelligent or passionate or capable) as you," or "Please help me, no one else understands." Both men and women can fall prey to these statements, hoping to make a real difference in someone else's life. Certainly contributing to the lives of others is a valued part of healthy relating, but people who perceive themselves as powerless make us feel like goddesses or supermen, more powerful and wonderful and, ultimately, obligated than we've felt before. Because of how seductive this can be, it is hard to tell the difference between falling into the Victim Trap and genuinely falling in love.

224

Men are especially vulnerable to females who believe they are powerless, usually underestimating the damage these women can cause. Since our society promotes the distortion that men are stronger than women, many men believe they can "control" or "manage" the women in their lives. The fact is, women who appear to be helpless can be extremely powerful and dangerous. Both women and men are powerful and neither are able to truly control the other.

Romantic relationships can prove to be some of the most dangerous relationships of all the Victim Traps. Movies and plays like *Fatal Attraction* and *Phantom of the Opera* have depicted these relationships, displaying the destructive power of the victim-mistress and the abused man who becomes hurtful to the woman he loves.

The truth is, relationships in the Victim Trap are attractive because we see some part of ourselves in the neediness of the other. We know what it's like to feel powerless, and it makes us feel good to think we can do something about helping someone else who might feel that way. We get stuck in the Victim Trap not because we're really trying to help the other person but because we are trying to heal our own unconscious feelings of powerlessness.

It is not helpful to criticize yourself for getting into dysfunctional relationships, but it is helpful to understand how you got there if you ever want to change. With all of our emphasis on the Victim Trap as being stuck in the past, you might get the impression that it's some kind of defect if you still find yourself feeling old feelings you thought you had worked through. The fact is, even after all you have learned you are still going to be attracted to familiar patterns of relating, at the same time as you are trying to change. The mind and body remember. Old pain can be revived if the circumstances are similar enough. This is nature's way of giving you a warning signal of danger. Brain patterns never go away completely, they just fade from lack of use. The goal is not to erase them but to create new patterns based on new ways of relating that become more dominant. That "Oh no, not again" feeling does not mean you didn't do your work before, it just means that the stuff you're going through now is abusive enough to revive those old feelings. The point is, now you can choose new responses.

There are many helpful questions to ask yourself in your efforts to better understand yourself and to grow. However, some questions will take you offtrack and waste your time. Avoid questions that imply self-blame such as, "Why didn't I see this coming?" "Why did I let this person get me involved in this mess?" or "Why didn't I take better care of myself?" While you need to learn from your choices in order not to repeat them, criticizing yourself is counterproductive.

Questions that blame others are also not helpful: "How could he do this to me?" "Why didn't she love me?" or "Why can't he do what he promised?" None of these questions will help you learn from the past. To the contrary, these questions will tie you more strongly to the past and to the person who hurt you.

Instead, ask yourself nonblaming questions that will facilitate your learning from past experiences. These may include:

▶ "If I were to do this over again, what would I do differently?"
▶ "What are the signs that, if I see them in another relationship, will signal me something is amiss?"
▶ "How did I handle this situation well?"
▶ "What boundaries do I need to set in this relationship and in others like it?"
▶ "How do I underestimate my power, or the power of others?"

226

Power is the ability to do or act. It can be used for growth or for destruction, so we must take responsibility for how we utilize power in our lives. When properly managed, power moves us forward, creating positive change in our lives.

CAPACITY FOR CHANGE

Most of us resist change, especially if we don't feel we're in control of that change. This is important to remember as you set realistic expectations for the future of your relationships. When you embrace more of your personal power and set boundaries that are healthier for you, it is common for the other party in the relationship to resist these changes. In fact, setting new boundaries can, initially, stir up more conflict than resolution. This conflict can be motivated by several unconscious issues supported by the Victim Trap.

First, the changes you make in your own behavior and boundaries can trigger a variety of emotions in the other person, such as fear, anger, grief, and, of course, powerlessness. Since people who believe they are powerless tend to mismanage these emotions, it is unwise to expect people in the Victim Trap to respond in a validating manner.

Second, since these same people often doubt their perceptions and abilities, they often have an exaggerated drive to convince others of their reality. Some will bring other people into your life who "agree" with them in an attempt to force you to give up your power and collude with them. Some will pursue you with renewed zeal, terrified that your perceptions about them may be accurate and wanting to talk you out of your new boundaries. Others will try to sabotage change indirectly through passive-aggressive behaviors such as refusing to talk things out with you directly, gossiping about you, or giving you "the silent treatment."

Third, relationships in the Victim Trap resist change because as you make healthier, more empowered choices for yourself, other people are confronted with taking more responsibility for their own actions. Since powerless people do not feel capable of managing their own lives, no matter how competent they may seem on the surface, it is natural for them to want to avoid growth. If the person in your life is unwilling to take advantage of the opportunity you give him or her to grow, expect an energetic attack as a response.

All this sounds like bad news, doesn't it? Well, at first the cure can seem worse than the disease. But we urge you to continue sorting through the muddle. Keep moving toward the light of day. Be kind to yourself through this process, recognizing that it is normal to be confused when you are making your own personal changes. Use your support network to help you develop realistic expectations about what you can receive from this relationship and how much change you can reasonably expect. Ask yourself questions like these:

1. In what ways have I had unrealistic expectations?
2. What areas in my life can I change?
3. What is the limit of my influence over others?
4. What is the extent of other people's power?
5. What is in their power to change?
6. Based on past behavior, what degree of change can realistically be expected?
7. What is reasonable, based on past experience, to expect from my relationships right now?
8. What is reasonable, based on past experience, to expect from my relationships in the future?

As you continue to utilize your support network for guidance, new options and more clarity often emerge. You will gain strength the more you set and defend healthy boundaries. Some who will not leave the Victim Trap will, upon realizing you will not return to old dysfunctional patterns, retreat and find someone else to take your place in the relationship. Others will continue to bait you, but as you grow you will less likely be pulled back into an unhealthy dynamic. It may take time, but eventually your hard work will pay off and your valuable energy and time will be channeled into healthier, more satisfying relationships where a shared reality is possible.

CAPACITY FOR RESOLUTION

Since most of us fall somewhere on a continuum of personal power, we'd find ourselves completely alone if we only related to people who were always perfectly powerful. Most of the relationships we encounter are a mixture of powerfulness and powerlessness and fall somewhere in the middle of the continuum. However, occasionally you will encounter a person who adamantly embraces a powerless stance and intends to remain there no matter what you say, do, or feel. So how do you deal with these people in your life?

Realize that you will never be fully satisfied if you choose to stay in a relationship caught in the Victim Trap. Some people are not able to come to long-term resolution. While you may be fooled into thinking progress has been made, you will soon be disappointed as past patterns reemerge. Consequently, it is important to learn how to tolerate feeling unsuccessful in relationships. One thing that has helped us when dealing with people who believe they are powerless is to remind ourselves that no matter what we do or change, it will never be enough to make them happy or make them change. While we have control over ourselves, we cannot control others. So we might as well set our own boundaries, give what we feel good about giving, and learn not to get defensive if we are told we are bad, insufficient, or uncaring.

One reason people get stuck in unproductive responses to their pain is because they have made a habit of simply "getting rid of it" rather than resolving it. Merely withdrawing from a relationship is one of the greatest mistakes anyone can make, because sometimes withdrawal is based on the belief that it can end a relationship's effects. If we cut off our feelings about someone, make sure we will never have any physical contact with that person again, and do our best to rid ourselves of any thoughts about the person, we can fool ourselves into believing we have ended the relationship. To reassure ourselves we are safe from danger, we say things like, "That's over and done with now, I don't even want to talk about it anymore" or "It's all in the past" or "That will never happen again." Unfortunately, these statements are based on the erroneous belief that if we stop consciously thinking about something, it no longer exists. This is similar to when small children close their eyes and think you can no longer see them.

"Ending" a relationship without redefining what it means to you is an illusion that will leave you in danger of continued abuse. Redefining a relationship is a solution that will empower you to go on to a new, more loving future. The problem is not whether we think about a relationship, but how we think about it. Some end relationships with the false belief that the pain will stop. They are then surprised when the nightmares continue or they end up in other relationships exactly like the last one.

This is not to imply that in some instances, cutting off all physical contact may not be necessary to protect yourself from further abuse. Sometimes people you're trying to leave behind will try to sabotage your efforts in a variety of ways. They may try to bait you into reconnecting with them by harassing you from afar. For example, they may try to engage you through gossip, by sending you letters, or making harassing phone calls. If at all possible, ignore these attempts to anger or upset you.

Others may engage in activities that cannot be ignored, such as breaking into your house, filing a lawsuit against you, stalking you, coming to your place of employment and causing a scene, or physically threatening you. Calling on support from friends, family, law enforcement and other public assistance agencies may be necessary to provide you with the protection you need.

Remember, some people who claim to be powerless can become powerfully hurtful, and you need to be prepared to protect yourself. These people do not believe they are powerful enough to live without you, so your skill at setting boundaries can cause them to become so afraid they will retaliate viciously. Their feeling that you are cutting them off can even result in violent attacks on you. Knowing how to effectively say goodbye is especially important in these cases. Be prepared to make use of your support network and the resources around you to keep you safe.

Once you have achieved physical separation, you still have the work of redefining the relationship in your life. Changing the meaning of abusive events, taking back your personal power, and developing a shared reality with those around you are some of the tools you will need. Don't be fooled into thinking that physically separating yourself from someone who mismanages power actually ends the relationship. You have the power to redefine relationships and the responsibility to set the boundaries exactly as you want them to be.

In these difficult situations, make sure to ask for help. No one can effectively cope with abuse or deprivation alone. Some people have lost belief in others, because no one was there to help them when they needed it. Needing others is not a sign of a weakness; it is a display of power that makes humans the strongest species on earth. Powerful people have powerful relationships, and they know how to manage their emotions to keep their relationships strong. Accountability, responsibility, and forgiveness are the tools that lead to relationships of interdependence and strength. No emotion is too threatening to face if we do not have to face it alone.

CAPACITY TO MANAGE EMOTIONS

To be free of the Victim Trap, we must learn how to manage our own emotions. We can determine what is a safe distance between ourselves and others only by knowing how we really feel about them. We must do the work of uncovering the feelings buried in our unconscious and in our bodies. Understanding the deeper emotions beneath our surface emotions is crucial to staying free from the Victim Trap. Awareness of the full range of our emotional responses to the people in our lives gives us the information we need to hold people accountable. Assessing the real danger means knowing the real emotions behind our responses to others.

Once we've been abused, we never have an easy time trusting others. But we can reclaim our ability to trust others as we reclaim trust in ourselves. Trusting our own emotions provides us with the information we need to assess another's trustworthiness. However, this is no simple task once we have been hurt.

Refusing to settle for a superficial understanding of our experiences with others means we refuse to believe we are powerless in relationships and we maintain the responsibility to examine ourselves and others to learn what we need to know to protect ourselves. As we face our pain, we gain the confidence to manage whatever emotions we have in order to hold others accountable and resolve unfinished business that may come up from the past.

If you are trying to break free from the Victim Trap, you will be tested by your emotions as you endeavor to turn your pain into power. Feelings of vulnerability, shame, rejection, and loneliness will find their way into your life, sometimes at the most inopportune times. Since a relationship caught in the Victim Trap can make you feel very needed, important, and even adored when things are going well, don't be fooled by this seduction. You are powerful, but not powerful enough to save, fix, rescue, control, or make someone else completely happy. Facing your own emotions includes grappling with the limits of your power as well as reclaiming what personal power is actually yours.

CAPACITY TO FORGIVE

If you've been in a relationship caught in the Victim Trap, then you have been hurt. Forgiveness is a necessary part of making peace with this relationship. Keep in mind that forgiveness is for you, not them. Forgiveness is an act of power, redefining your identity and allowing you to look into the future instead of the past. Rather than a one-time event, forgiveness is a dynamic, ongoing process.

Simple to understand, forgiveness is very difficult to accomplish. To begin, you must make the decision not to return hurt for hurt. Revenge can appear so satisfying that we can easily delude ourselves into believing that hurting those who hurt us is an act of justice. We have found the counsel of others extremely helpful during this emotional time. Revenge may seem sweet for a moment, but you will suffer just as much as the person you hurt. By returning hurt for hurt, you throw yourself back into the Victim Trap. Talking about revenge, contained and cathartic, may be helpful in some situations. But when it's time to act, invest energy into setting and enforcing appropriate boundaries.

If possible, talk with the person who has hurt you to come to a common understanding of how you have been injured. It is preferable if the one who has offended you understands your feelings. Sometimes, this is not possible. You can use your support network to confront your pain with or without the cooperation of the one who hurt you. There are people around you right now who can enter into a shared reality with you. Having your painful feelings deeply understood is important to achieve forgiveness.

There may be those you do not want to forgive or perhaps are not ready to forgive. If you need more time, do not rush yourself, but continue your process of recovery. Sometimes you may not want to forgive someone who has hurt you because they seemed to benefit from the pain in your life and you do not want them to be happy in any way now. You may mistakenly believe that forgiving them is saying it was okay for them to do what they did to you. This is never true. Forgiveness just means you are breaking free of their negative hold on your life and moving on toward happiness, no matter what anyone else does.

If someone asks for your forgiveness, never say, "That's okay," because hurting you wasn't acceptable. Only after you believe he or she understands how deeply you have been hurt, and is genuinely sorry for having caused this pain and takes action to make amends, can you honestly say, "I forgive you."

Forgiveness is not an invitation to begin a new relationship, but a statement that something very wrong has been acknowledged and put behind you. Many people misunderstand forgiveness as meaning you must allow the person who has hurt you to return into your life. This is not so. There are some people, even though you have forgiven them, who are not safe for you. You don't need to hold resentments toward others to keep them out of your life. You have the power to forgive them and move on, which for some people in your past, means moving on without them present.

If you never have the opportunity to resolve things directly with the person who has harmed you, you can still forgive. Part of the healing in your life may come when you stop seeing the other's happiness as "about you." This means you were not responsible for his or her happiness in the past and you are not responsible for it now. Wanting someone never to be happy because you were hurt keeps you unhappy. This person remains in a place of importance in your life. While you may choose this option, it consumes energy you may need to move on to loving relationships in your future. Remember, your anger exists to protect you and correct problems in your life, not to violate someone else, as if human suffering could be measured and evenly balanced. If a hurtful person has moved through your life and appears to be happy now, it is not "about you" anymore. Having new, healthy, mutually satisfying relationships is.

ESCAPING THE VICTIM TRAP

We have said many times that none of us is perfect, so none of us has perfect relationships. Be kind with yourself as you assess your relationships, without falling off either end of the continuum. Be careful not to withdraw from meaningful relationships when you notice the slightest flaw. Perfectionistic attitudes will lead to loneliness. At the same time, be cautious not to stay unprotected in dangerous relationships by staying actively involved long after closure is called for. Embrace your personal power and allow the process of healing love to flourish in your life.

ACKNOWLEDGMENTS

WE ARE GRATEFUL for the significant contributions many people have made to the development of this project.

Appreciation is extended to the therapists at the La Vie Center and Lauri Hughes, the office manager, for providing personal support as well as helpful consultations to Mark throughout this process; and to Dr. Robert Stolorow and the members of the Thursday evening study group for contributing to Mark's theoretical understanding of the psychology of victimization.

Special thanks goes to the Task Force for Men's Ministry at Bel Air Presbyterian Church and The Men from the Mountain for their contribution to Mark's spiritual development (a work-in-progress) and their unconditional love.

Heartfelt gratitude is extended to the staff and board members of the ministries of Christian Recovery International for providing Carmen with personal support, theological understanding, and ample opportunity to face her ambivalence about power.

We appreciate the empowerment we've received from our therapists: Dr. Rita Resnick, Dr. Bernard Brickman, Dr. Paul Roberts, and Victor Parra, LCSW. In addition, Carmen is grateful for the healing touch of her body work and massage therapists: Carolyn Braddock, Claudette Renner, Mandy Stephen, Charles Swan, Carlos Rivera, Karen Gruszynski, and Stephen Jones.

We thank our families, especially our parents, Charles K. Baker and Patricia Diane Baker, Dr. David A. Berry and Mary

Ellen Berry, for making unique contributions to the people we've become today.

For personal support and love throughout the writing process, we want to thank Barbara Rauen, Dwight Case, Don and Simone Morgan, Mack Harnden, J. D. Hinton and Mimi Craven, Tim Swift, Gary and Thereza Verboon, Ellen Rhoda, Joe Venema, Lynn Barrington, Joel Miller, Gail Walker, Pat Luehers, Connie Lillas, Trevor Dobbs, Dale Ryan, Jim Kermath, Irene Flores, Rene Chansler, Bobette Buster, Coleen Friend, Bob Myers, Dan Psaute, Christopher Knippers, Leon Bass, John Kitzmiller, David and Wendy Wilkinson, Susan Latta, Dale and Sara Wolery, Lori Wolery, Virginia and John Frederich, Marianne Croonquist, Sandy Wilson, Jack McGinnis, Diana Loomis, and (last but not least) Stephen Smith. We are especially grateful for the entertainment and comfort received from our cats, Harley, Scooter, Sassy, and Stud, who refuse to be powerless in any human exchange.

We give special thanks to Roy M. Carlisle, senior editorial consultant at Piñon Press, for recognizing the need for this project, providing invaluable editorial support, carefully reviewing the manuscript in its many versions, and refereeing the balance of power between the authors.

We are also grateful to Jean Blomquist who brought her strong professional skills as a copyeditor to this project in those final days when every author worries about whether the book is really complete. With Jean's help we finally did finish the manuscript, much to the surprise of many.

No book ever sees the light of day nor does it ever reach the hands of readers without the dedication and work of the whole publishing team, and we want to thank the Piñon Press team, John, for keeping the vision alive; Erik, for his loyalty and marketing tenacity; Traci, for her editorial help and project oversight; Toben, Jorge, Diane, Kasha, and all the others within the publishing house who have patiently maintained their enthusiasm for this project.

AUTHORS

CARMEN RENEE BERRY, MSW, MA, is a nationally certified massage and body worker, social worker, and former psychotherapist. She instructs persons of all ages on how to integrate the body-mind-spirit into a journey toward wholeness. Ms. Berry promotes healthy lifestyles for stressed and distressed people through her many workshops, seminars, articles, and books.

Currently, Ms. Berry is director of The Next Step, which offers body-friendly services and resources. She is the author of six books, including the best-selling *When Helping You Is Hurting Me*, *Are You Having Fun Yet?*, *Your Body Never Lies*, and *Girlfriends*, which she coauthored with Tamara Traeder. Her articles have appeared in numerous professional, popular, and religious magazines.

Ms. Berry is a graduate of the University of Southern California's School of Social Work and has an MA in Social Sciences from Northern Arizona University. She resides in Pasadena, California. Ms. Berry can be contacted at:

The Next Step
259 N. Holliston, Suite 3
Pasadena, California 91106
(818)578-1279

DR. MARK W. BAKER has received his PhD in Clinical Psychology, and his Master's Degree in Theology. He is licensed as a Clinical Psychologist as well as a Marriage, Family, and Child Counselor. Dr. Baker is the Executive Director of the La Vie Center in Pasadena, a whole-person health-care center that specializes in treating the body, mind and spirit. He also has a private practice in Santa Monica, California. Dr. Baker has published several articles in professional journals, and leads numerous workshops each year on spiritual and psychological growth. He has appeared on television and radio to facilitate healthier relationships through teaching the basic principles of self-esteem and greater intimacy between men and women. For a list of Dr. Baker's tapes on personal growth, you may contact him at:

The La Vie Center
650 Sierra Madre Villa, Suite 110
Pasadena, California 91107
(818)351-9616